From the "backroom-boy" who hopped inside the bunk to a "backroom-girl" who knows the experience

[signature]

(husband of Meg)

WHAT THE PROFESSIONALS ARE SAYING

For the past ten years, Dr. Margaret Patterson has tenaciously followed a lead, derived from her early experience with acupuncture, that indicated a profound relationship between very low level, pulsating, electrical currents and the workings of the human brain. In addition to the basic knowledge and insight into mental mechanisms gained from her research she has developed an extraordinarily successful clinical treatment for the addictive disorders.

At this time, I know of no other treatment procedure with as low a rate of recidivism, nor any other method which is so devoid of the production of physiological signs of withdrawal. NET may well be not only the optimal method for the treatment of such conditions, but may have a similar utility in other areas of psychiatry and may well prove to be a forerunner of other applications of bioelectric therapy.

—**Robert O. Becker, M.D.,** *consultant in biomedical sciences, former director of research in bioelectricity, Veterans Administration Hospital, Syracuse, N.Y.*

I was fascinated with the book and quite excited by the possibility of a new tool for fighting drug addiction. When a person with Christian faith accepts the discipline of scientific inquiry, the value of both the science and the faith is enhanced. They belong together and they are together in Dr. Patterson's book.

—**Dr. Paul Brand,** *professor of surgery, Louisiana State University, and coauthor of* Fearfully and Wonderfully Made

---

It's so simple. . . . It's a little metal box with leads that clip onto your ears and in two or three days—which is the worst period for kicking junk—in these 72 hours it leaves your system. Actually you should be incredibly sick, but for some reason you're not. Why? I don't know, because all it is is a very simple, nine-volt, battery-run operation.

—Keith Richards, *of the rock group Rolling Stones*

Dr. Patterson's book *Getting Off the Hook* is totally engrossing, sensitive and right on target in defining the relevant personal and societal parameters that underly the epidemic misuse of consciousness-altering drugs. Her approach to patients is refreshingly wholistic, integrating body, mind, and spirit. Her delineation of the spiritual dimensions of treatment is particularly welcome, as it expresses a point of view that often is disregarded by conventional medicine. Her study of . . . stimulation for addiction treatment is part of a revolution in the use of electricity for treating a wide range of medical and psychiatric disorders.

—Richard B. Resnick, M.D., *associate professor of psychiatry, New York Medical College*

Dr. Patterson's most important contributions to our understanding of the nature of electrotherapy are her observations of the dependence of the specific, therapeutic effect on the frequency and exact form of electrical current. This discovery offers enormous potential for treatment not only of addictions but also of other diseases.

Getting Off the Hook is unique in describing a physical means of eliminating this dreadful affliction of modern society, as well as the generally ignored spiritual nature of man and the intricate relationship of body and mind.

—Boguslaw Lipinski, Ph.D., *president, International Society for Bioelectricity*

Meg Patterson's work is a revolution in curing addiction. Her approach is a revolution, too, but no mystery. She uses NeuroElectric Therapy techniques.

—Pete Townshend, *leader of the British rock band, The Who*

How wonderful it is to come upon one who really cares and who can really help. I have known Meg Patterson, a most able Scotswoman, for some ten years since first we met in Hong Kong. A healer at heart by training and practice, she addresses herself to the greatest problem of all today—addiction. Her experiences revealed the tool with which to handle addictions and, recognizing the call, the compulsion of conscience and commitment, she follows the lead and moves to ever deeper understanding and ability with the precision of craftsmanship and the inspiration of enlightenment and love. Only public and governmental lethargy and blind exploitation of pain and misery stand in the way of her approach—as spiritual as it is psychological, as rational as it is compassionate. As with the greatest advances in knowledge, this overwhelming advance can reverse the lamentable trend of our civilization, by a process of healing, of health, and of hope.

—Yehudi Menuhin, *internationally-famous violinist*

Misuse of drugs is America's most severe social problem. Dr. Patterson may have here a long-awaited answer.

She states clearly that NET is not a cure for addiction; it's a detoxification process. But that's a key step towards rehabilitation; it's a door to release from this literal prison. Then the mind can be transformed and the underlying problems solved. That is society's hope. This book is worth your reading.

—Herbert E. Ellingwood, *former deputy counsel to the President of the United States*

This book should be standard reading in any modern educational system.

—Sean Connery, *internationally-known film actor*

A fascinating personal odyssey by an intelligent and independent-minded physician dedicated to helping those afflicted with drug addiction. The writing is lucid, and the style light; but there are sufficient hard data and bibliographic references to please even the serious scholar. Dr. Patterson leads us along the interesting course of development of her own views and practical approaches to drug detoxification through NeuroElectric Therapy.

—**Dr. John C. Liebeskind,** *professor, department of psychology, UCLA*

Dr. Patterson has developed a physical method for utilizing the brain's own reserve capacity to overcome drug withdrawal. She demonstrates her mastery of the science of addiction but also her sensitivity to the addicts, many of whom suffer for years after successfully giving up drugs. NET and other endorphinogenic treatments could offer great promise in returning past addicts to full function.

—**Mark S. Gold, M.D.,** *director of research, Fair Oaks Hospital, Summit, N.J.*

GETTING OFF THE HOOK

GETTING OFF THE HOOK

Addictions Can Be Cured by NET (NeuroElectric Therapy)

Dr. Meg Patterson

Fellow of the Royal College of Surgeons, Edinburgh

Harold Shaw Publishers
Wheaton, Illinois

Printed in the United States of America

Library of Congress Cataloging in Publication Data

Patterson, Meg, 1923-
  Getting off the hook.

  Bibliography: p.
  Includes index.
    1. Drug abuse—Treatment. 2. Electric shock therapy.
I. Title. [DNLM: 1. Substance dependence—Therapy.
2. Electrotherapy. 3. Acupuncture. WM 270 P318g]
RC564.P37 1983   616.86'0645   83-10862
ISBN 0–87788–305–X

First printing, July 1983

To Lorne, Sean, and Myrrh
for sharing all the struggles with patience,
understanding, and, now, their lives

"*Bait:* A preparation that renders the hook more palatable. The best kind is beauty."
—Ambrose: *The Devil's Dictionary*

"Come live with me, and be my love,
And we will some new pleasures
    prove
Of golden sands, and crystal brooks,
With silken lines, and silver hooks."
—John Donne: *The Bait*

"To be hooked: . . . More recently it also means addicted to the use of a drug."
—*Bartlett's Familiar Quotations*

addict: addictus: past participle: *addicere:* to favor, to adjudge. (i) to award by judicial decree; (ii) to surrender, to attach oneself as a follower to a person, or adherent to a cause; (iii) to surrender as a constant practice, *e.g.,* "we sincerely addict ourselves to Almighty God." Thomas Fuller.
—Webster's Dictionary

PREFACE

This book is about healing people of their addictions to various kinds of drugs. The title comes from two British Broadcasting Corporation television documentaries, "Off the Hook" (1975) and "Still Off the Hook" (1977). The two films followed an officially registered drug addict from the first day of his NeuroElectric Therapy (NET) to the tenth day, then presented a profile of the same individual two years later. A third BBC-TV documentary about NET, "The Black Box," produced by a scientific rather than a human interest film unit, was broadcast in February 1981.

The book is divided into Parts I, II, and III which follow the logical sequence required in dealing with the subject of addictions. I addresses the medical and scientific problems associated with detoxification of substance abuse; II describes the psycho-spiritual problems contributing to the habit, requiring psycho-therapeutic rehabilitation during and after detoxification; III highlights the necessity for these to be brought together in a treatment program not hitherto practiced. Readers may choose the part that is most relevant to their particular field of interest.

There is a curious dichotomy associated with the word "cure" when applied to addictions—even by doctors. When the question of cure is raised in conditions other than addictions—the common cold or hepatitis for example—it is usually taken by all concerned to mean the temporary resolution of the condition. That is, the cold is treated with medication and disappears for a month or a year, when it may appear again; and the hepatitis is treated and may reappear if the patient again uses dirty needles. Such qualifications are rarely considered by doctors, patients, and general public when the subject is the cure of addictions, where it is taken by all to mean "a total cure of all signs of the condition, with no possible recurrence no matter what the patient chooses to do."

However, in this book the word "cure" may be defined in two ways. One, the process of *detoxification* from all substance abuse which can be achieved quickly and with a minimal amount of discomfort, according to all acceptable definitions of "cure"—medical, scientific, and statistical. However, if the addiction condition is expanded to include contributory psycho-spiritual causes, then a number of other factors must be included as criteria in defining "cure." Some of these are dealt with in Part II, "Re-defining Addictions."

The definition of cure for which I would prefer to be judged is: "The healing in body, mind and spirit, of those who were previously unable to function responsibly because of substance abuse. This would involve a comprehension and a demonstrated capacity to put into effect a new philosophy of life which is adequate to their chosen environment so that they are no longer in bondage to a chemical or behavioral addiction, but can live with freedom, joy, and love in family and community."

The treatment of chemical-substance abuse portrayed in the three BBC-TV documentaries, and described in this book, is a demonstrably successful form of therapy discovered in Hong Kong and developed in England. Yet the three documentaries also revealed a conspicuous disinterest in NeuroElectric Therapy by the British government. To develop NET to its present state I have had to turn to private citizens and to private industry for support.

I am grateful to the many scientists who have encouraged and advised me. I also wish to render thanks to The Rank Foundation for funding the clinical trial at the Pharmakon Clinic in Sussex; to the Clinic Staff for their dedication and enthusiasm; to the Marie Curie Memorial Foundation Research Department for their invaluable work with NET in animal models; to *Omni* magazine for permission to reproduce an article on NET and especially to the author, Kathleen McAuliffe, for her long and painstaking research before she decided that NET was a valid treatment which should be publicized; to all my patients—for each one of you has taught me something about NET and life; to many friends who have given us practical support and encouragement, particularly the rock music group The Who, and to their leader Pete Townshend for his courage in speaking publicly of his own problems and of his treatment by NET with openness and insight; to Gordon H. Crowther for helping to make the treatment available to the world; to Luci Shaw, my editor, for her skilled editing and patient understanding; and, most of all, to my husband George, for his unfailing support and inspiration and his contributions to several chapters.

Corona del Mar, California　　　　　　　　　　　　　　Meg Patterson
April, 1983　　　　　　　　　M.B.E., MB.Ch.B., (= M.D.), F.R.C.S.E.

CHRONOLOGY OF MAIN EVENTS
THAT LED TO THE DISCOVERY
AND DEVELOPMENT OF NET

1964

Arrival in Hong Kong. Surgery appointment.

1972

President Nixon's visit to China and worldwide publicity for acupuncture.
Dr. Wen visits China to study electro-acupuncture.
Electro-acupuncture found to cure drug addictions.

1973

Dr. Irving Cooper's visit to Hong Kong which increased my interest in electrical stimulation.
Dr. Robert Becker's work with electrical stimulation of bone tissue reported in media.
Reports of Dr. Snyder and Dr. Pert's discovery of opiate receptors in the brain.
Dr. Liebeskind's discovery that pain sensation may be diminished by electrical stimulation of certain areas of the brain in animals.,
Treatment of one hundred drug addicts in Hong Kong by electro-acupuncture.
Realization that there is a significant difference between electro-acupuncture and NET. Decision to concentrate on NET.
Decision to return to London, leave surgery, and research NET in depth.
Establishment of private practice on Harley Street, initiation of research on NET, and application to Medical Research Council for grant to perform double-blind trial of NET. Failure to get sufficient funds.

1974

Treatment of Eric Clapton, with subsequent wide publicity.
Financial support received from rock music groups and Yehudi Menuhin to continue NET research.
Development of first "Shackman-Patterson" NET stimulators.
Growth of conviction that rapid rehabilitation must follow rapid detoxifica-

tion. George begins systematic research and program development.

Intensive investigation of electronics, biology, neuro-electrical stimulation, symptoms, and treatment of addictions to all chemicals producing altered states of consciousness, and their significance.

1975

Visits to European conferences; visit to U.S.A.; meeting with Dr. Cooper and Dr. Becker and with the Institute for the Study of Human Issues.

Shooting for first BBC-TV documentary "Off the Hook" showing daily treatment of heroin addict and resultant detoxification.

Writing of "Interim Report: Addictions Can Be Cured," published in England.

Drs. Kosterlitz and Hughes' announcement of discovery of endorphins one month after publication of book.

Visit to Dr. Kosterlitz in Aberdeen for discussions regarding electrical stimulation, NET, my "Chemical X" and endorphins.

Rethinking of whole area of treatment of addictions in light of discovery of endorphins and their function.

1976

Research continued; patients treated; different models of machines tested.

Research grants sought in U.K. and U.S.A.

1977

Filming of second BBC-TV documentary "Still Off the Hook."

Treatment of Keith Richards in U.S.A.

Discussions with State (New Jersey) and Federal (Washington) officials regarding use of NET in their clinics. Decision to move to U.S.A.

Showing of second BBC-TV film in U.K. produces finances for NET clinical trials in U.K. Decision to postpone move to U.S.A.

Development of new models of "Pharmakon-Patterson" stimulator with European Electronic Systems.

1978

Preparations to set up Pharmakon Clinic combining NET detoxification and rehabilitation—the first of its kind anywhere.

Joint research project initiated with Marie Curie Memorial Foundation Research Laboratories to investigate NET in laboratory animals.

Appropriate staff personnel sought and training materials prepared for Pharmakon Clinic.

1979

Preparation of new Model IV NET stimulator for use in Pharmakon Clinic.

Move to Pharmakon Clinic quarters in Broadhurst Manor to prepare for patients, negotiate official permits, prepare all paper-work, and ready training programs.

1980

Clinical trial held in Pharmakon Clinic, January-December.

1981

Commencement of follow-up research of patients treated over seven years in U.K.

Departure for U.S.A. in March to launch NET there and worldwide.

1982

MEGNET Model V stimulator designed. Work done on materials for publication.

Completion of seven year follow-up research and statistical analysis of findings.

1983

NeuroElectric Therapy Incorporated set up to market and distribute MEGNET stimulators worldwide.

Meg Patterson Research Foundation set up to research further use of electro-stimulation in therapy for diseases and conditions other than addictions.

Franchise for national and international Pharmakon Clinics prepared, based on psycho-spiritual program developed for original Pharmakon Clinic in U.K.

PART I
DETOXIFYING
ADDICTIONS

1 ADDICTS AND NET

Keith Richards, the world-famous "bad boy" rock music star of the Rolling Stones, with a notoriously heavy drug addiction problem, said: "It's so simple it's not true...It's a little metal box with leads that clip on to your ears and in two or three days—which is the worst period for kicking junk—in these seventy-two hours it leaves your system. Actually, you should be incredibly sick, but for some reason you're not. Why? I don't know, because all it is is a very simple, nine-volt, battery-run operation."

Eric Clapton, the world's greatest blues guitarist, who was unable to perform for several years because of his drug addiction, said: "I wasn't actually looking for a cure...It made me stop wanting to take smack."

Pete Townshend, leader of what has been called "the greatest rock-and-roll band in the world," The Who, said: "Meg Patterson's work is a revolution in curing addiction. Her approach is a revolution, too, but no mystery. She uses NeuroElectric Therapy techniques..."

These are only three of the many testimonials to NeuroElectric Therapy (NET) from internationally-known rock music stars who had serious problems with chemical substance addictions, were cured of those addictions, and, several years later, are still performing on the world stage, free of their habit. They are well-known public figures who have spoken to the media on many occasions about their addictions and treatment by NET; there is thus no breach of medical ethics in using their names here. Because the identities of many others who have been treated for addictions must be safeguarded, I will be using pseudonyms in describing their conditions.

Sam was a twenty-four-year-old heroin addict. He had smoked or snorted about 2 grams daily for four years, as well as a gram or more of cocaine daily for eleven years (he had a large hole in his nasal septum from this habit); every day for six months he had taken 5,000 milligrams of the barbiturate Tuinal, and 20 tablets of Paracetamol (acetaminophen, or Tylenol in the U.S.A.). The Paracetamol was for the excruciating headaches which had developed from his excessive drug abuse. Because these headaches were so severe I sent him to be investigated for a possible brain tumor, but none was found. On his admission I stopped all drugs immediately, and except for one brief convulsion of a few seconds' duration on the fifth day of treatment he had no further trouble. All headaches had disappeared by the time he was discharged three weeks later.

Just as the problem of diabetes needed reassessment after the development of insulin, or Parkinson's disease after L-dopa, the whole problem of addictions must be reassessed in the light of recent scientific discoveries and psychotherapeutic experience. Addiction is a much more serious problem than these, or most other, illnesses. Alcoholism is America's second-worst health problem (after heart disease), affecting one in every ten persons; and cigarette smoking is, according to a recent U.S. government pamphlet, "the most widespread example of drug dependence," with 56 million addicts "because nicotine reinforces and strengthens the desire to smoke and causes the users to keep on smoking."[1]

Johnny, thirty, had been an alcoholic for ten years, but only on week-ends because during the week his job required skill and concentration. For eight years he had been taking up to 100 milligrams of Valium daily, legally prescribed by his doctor, for his bouts of "depression." On Valium he was increasingly losing control, was anxious, bad-tempered, dysphoric. When he tried to stop the Valium by himself he felt a paralyzing sense of "plunging into a bottomless pit." With NET he came off both alcohol and Valium eas ily, with no convulsions, and only one night of poor sleep. Ten months later he wrote: "I cannot say how grateful we all are for my treatment. It unveiled an unknown quality in myself of loving and caring for my family."

As I write this, the national NBC-TV network has just aired a program on teenage alcoholism in which it was stated that there is an alcohol-related traffic accident every twenty-one minutes. More Americans die every year through alcohol-related circumstances than died in the whole Vietnam War. Drugs cost industry $25 billion each year, according to an interview in U.S.A. Today with Dr. Dale Masi, Director of the Office of Employee Counseling Sevices for the Department of Health and Human Services. Dr. Masi added:

"We estimate that 18 percent of any work population, not just the federal government, is suffering a 10 percent alcohol, or 2 to 3 percent drug problem and a good 6 to 7 percent emotional problems that affect productivity in the work place. It really becomes a good investment, both in human resources and money for a company, for an employer to have an employee counselling program. If you have 1,000 employees, we know that 18 percent, namely 180 of them, are losing productivity, 25 percent of that due to personal problems. For example, we estimate that in our Department of Health and Human Services, we have maybe 150,000 employees at an average salary of $22,000. So you come up with about $150 million in lost productivity yearly."[2]

Judy, fifty years of age, had smoked thirty cigarettes daily for thirty years. She had tried repeatedly to stop smoking by many methods, including hypnosis and "de-programming" but this only resulted in her becoming, in her own words, "a hysterical, raving lunatic." Immediately she was put on NET her cigarettes were stopped, and throughout the five-day treatment she was completely calm and relaxed, and slept well.

Figure 1 (next page) showing the breakdown of drug use among Americans over the age of twenty-six by type of drug (responses in percentages), was given by the National Institute on Drug Abuse, Washington, D.C.

President Reagan, in a nationally televised Press Conference on March

Drug	1974	1977	1979
Alcohol	73.2%	77.9%	91.5%
Cigarettes	65.4	67.0	83.0
Marijuana	9.9	15.3	19.6
Cocaine	0.9	2.6	4.3
Stimulants	3.0	4.7	5.8
Hallucinogens	1.3	2.6	4.5
Tranquilizers	2.0	2.6	3.1
Sedatives	2.0	2.4	3.5
Heroin	0.5	0.8	1.0

Figure 1: Results of NIDA survey of drug use by Americans over 26.

6, 1981, declared drug abuse "one of the greatest problems facing us internally in the United States." He concluded by saying "if something isn't done we're running the risk of losing a great part of a whole generation."

According to the *New England Journal of Medicine* of April 1983, one-fourth of the U.S. population has tried marijuana and twenty million people use it daily.[3] The White House Drug Abuse Policy Office reports (in a survey covering half a million students) that pressure to use marijuana and alcohol starts as early as fourth grade.[4]

Ann, fifty-one, began smoking hashish "in an attempt to relate better" to her hashish-smoking daughter, then found she could not stop. She had smoked 20 to 25 joints of hashish daily for seven years. She had also been drinking a quart of vodka daily for eight years. Two days after stopping the hashish on her own initiative she began suffering from very acute withdrawal symptoms. She responded rapidly to out-patient treatment by NET, which also returned her, for the first time in many years, to a normal sleep pattern.

The *Wall Street Journal,* in a front-page article, reported:
"Across the country, college and university officials are growing increasingly concerned about alcohol abuse among students. Believing it a far more dangerous and widespread problem than illegal drug use, more than half the nation's colleges in recent years have begun programs to combat excessive drinking by students.

"Yet so far such efforts have produced little more than a heightened sense of frustration among college officials. Instead of declining, student drinking problems at many campuses continue to increase. Worried administrators also report a rise in alcohol-related violence and vandalism...."[5]

*Nancy was a fifty-one year-old alcoholic who arrived at the clinic in a state of extreme intoxication. In addition to four bottles of sherry daily for one and one-half years she had been taking 40 milligrams of Valium daily for five years, 75 milligrams of Sinequan (doxepin, a tricyclic anti-depressant) daily for nine months, and 75 milligrams of Anafranil (clomipramine, a tri-cyclic anti-depressant) nightly for nine months. Despite this huge alcohol habit she had neither **delirium tremens** (a special form of delirium with terrifying delusions to which drinkers are liable), nor "the shakes." The alcohol craving disappeared on the third day of NET, and both appearance and behavior changed dramatically before discharge six weeks later.*

Dr. David Smith, the founder and medical director of the Haight-Ashbury Free Medical Clinic in San Francisco, said recently that increasing numbers of American middle-class cocaine users are now mixing it with heroin to modify the stimulant effects of cocaine, both by injection and free-basing. He also stated categorically that despite the claims of some researchers in earlier years cocaine had now emerged as "the most addictive drug" in popular use. This statement also reflects my own experience. In 1981 the Drug Abuse Warning Network, Project Dawn, a federally-funded drug research center outside Philadelphia, published drug statistics from twenty-six metropolitan areas throughout the United States demonstrating the serious increase in cocaine abuse and deaths (see figure 2 on next page).

Larry, forty-two, had been injecting heroin and cocaine intravenously in very large doses for twenty years. He was then transferred by his doctor to methadone tablets, and for five years before his NET treatment had been given 500 milligrams of methadone daily and legally by the same doctor. He had been hospitalized fifteen times in attempts to stop his addicition, without success, and he did not believe it was possible to be cured by electrical stimulation or any other means. After being successfully detoxified by NET he was still off all drugs two years later.

Cocaine-related deaths

	San Francisco	Chicago	Los Angeles	Miami	New York
1977	8	2	9	0	13
1978	4	6	10	28	10
1979	9	4	19	27	19
1980	10	9	26	56	79

Cocaine-related emergency room admissions

	San Francisco	Miami	New York
1977	41		
1978	51	29	168
1979	61	45	212
1980	87	54	683

Figure 2

Stress affects all kinds and classes of people, from highly paid company executives to rock musicians to housekeepers to teenagers. Almost every family has some member dependent on some chemical for some stress.

The symptoms of stress are well-known: anxiety, headaches, sleeplessness, irritation, sweaty palms, urge to urinate, memory blanks, mental and physical pain. The standard treatment for any of these symptoms is invariably a drug, the effects of which are often more serious than the stress condition itself. The problem of stress, and its solution, accounts for the largest financial investment in research by the wealthiest pharmaceutical companies in the world.

Our bodies are so constructed that every form of stress alerts the brain to produce a substance to deal with that impulse. For example, in war, or sport, or business, or during a family quarrel, when we feel anxiety, or stress, or fear, our brains—which were quietly ticking over at 8 to 12 cycles per second before the stress impulse—suddenly switch to a higher frequency of 13 to 21 cycles per second. This triggers certain cells to produce a natural chemical substance which helps us to meet and overcome the problem, such as adrenalin for "fight or flight" situations; or the recently discovered enkephalin, for circumstances involving pain or emotion.

Our brain cells have the capacity to produce all sorts of chemicals when required. But if, instead of meeting or resolving the problem, we panic or are defeated by such stress-inducing situations and run to the doctor (or cigarette vending-machine, or liquor store, or drug dealer, or pharmacist) for some form of synthetic chemical, and we introduce this to the body, the brain immediately gets the message and stops producing its own natural substance. Then, when we try to stop taking the medicine, or cigarette, or drug, or alcohol, we suffer a "drug hunger," or "withdrawal," or "craving." We are on our way to addiction.

Archie, at thirty-five, had been on cocaine for fourteen years, gradually increasing his habit to 5 grams daily at the time of admission to the clinic. He had also snorted 1 gram of heroin daily for ten years. He was terrified at the possibility of having no cocaine, for he had not been without it for a single day in two years. Six months after successful detoxification and discharge from NET treatment he told a gathering of doctors at a medical conference that NET had not only freed him from addiction but had brought about an actual change for the better in his character.

Time Magazine reported in 1981 that "if all the international dealers who supply the United States market—not even including the retailers—were to form a single corporation, it would probably rank seventh on the *Fortune* 500 list, between Ford Motor Company ($37 billion in revenue) and Gulf Oil Corporation ($26.5 billion)."[6] And in 1983 *Time* said that "among the 4 million to 5 million Americans who regularly use cocaine, drug counselors estimate that 5% to 20%—at least 200,000, perhaps 1 million—are now profoundly dependent on cocaine, a new corps as numerous as heroin addicts. . . During the past two years or so, the number of Americans who have used the drug climbed from 15 million to 20 million and is rising still: every day some 5,000 neophytes sniff a line of coke for the first time. . .Cocaine has become a $25 billion business, about three time as big as the recording and movie industries put together. Selling coke is, in the words of one U. S. drug official, 'the most lucrative of all underworld ventures.' "[7]

Mike, thirty-six, had been mainlining 2 grams of heroin daily for eight years, and often up to 10 grams a day when available. In addition, he was injecting methadone (Physeptone ampoules for I.V. use) 120 milligrams daily, and sometimes up to 500 milligrams a day; up to 10 grams of cocaine daily, often "free-basing" it, during the same period; and at night he took four tablets of Mandrax (methaqualone, or Quaaludes in the U.S.). Part of this huge drug intake was legally prescribed because he was a registered addict at a Government Drug Dependency Unit. All his superficial veins were thrombosed and unusable. For the eight months prior to admission for NET treatment he had been injecting drugs into his right femoral vein (in the groin) up to fifteen times a day. This area was a mass of thickened scars. I personally witnessed him insert a needle easily and unerringly when he withdrew a blood sample for testing because the nurses could not obtain it from a vein. He stated categorically he had no withdrawal symptoms at all with NET, and that his only complaint was not having a full night's sleep until the ninth night. The nursing staff reported he had no signs of withdrawal. His urine was checked at the end of the first week, and was negative for all drugs.

NET itself is not a cure for addiction. But it is an effective detoxification of addictions of all kinds—the first to be discovered. For centuries alcoholics, drug addicts, and drug dependents wishing to get off their drug have had to "dry out," or go "cold turkey," or even take another, more addictive drug as a supposed cure. Now, for the first time, it is possible for addicts to be detoxified from any chemical form of addiction, in only ten days, with minimal discomfort. NET is also the first treatment ever to reverse the long-term Chronic Withdrawal Syndrome, which lasts for many months, in addition to dealing with the Acute Withdrawal Syndrome.

This detoxification is accomplished by a pocket-size, transistorized machine. This machine, with its quadrillion possible combinations of frequencies and wave-forms, launches a new scientific system of medicine which no longer drugs the body with chemicals in treatment, but stimulates body cells to produce their own natural chemical substances.

The small, portable stimulator, similar in appearance to the transistor radio headphones worn by joggers, has two leads which attach to adhesive eletrodes fitted behind the ears. These carry the current, which gives a slight, not unpleasant tingling sensation while the patients go about their daily tasks.

Naturally, rehabilitation will be necessary for those who require a psycho-spiritual system to help them cope with the stress factors which made them addicts in the first place, but detoxification first needs to be successfully accomplished in those chemically addicted. This has been the major obstacle to successfully treating all forms of addiction—until NET. The MEGNET stimulator is not itself addictive. After ten days of treatment it has completed its work, no matter how large the dosage, the type of drug, or the duration of drug usage.

Sarah, twenty-two, was a registered drug addict who had been receiving 400 milligrams of pure (100%) heroin daily from a Government Drug Dependency Unit. She had begun mainlining 3 grams of street heroin at the age of seventeen, and the Government heroin replaced this. Every night she took "very large" doses of sedatives. In addition, she had taken 30 milligrams of linctus methadone daily for three years. Four hours before she was admitted for NET treatment she injected 900 milligrams of pure heroin intravenously and drank two one-pint bottles of linctus methadone. Her tolerance for drugs was so high she didn't even fall asleep, although her speech was slurred and her eyes glazed. She had only mild discomfort during her early treatment with NET, and was exercising enthusiastically within forty-eight hours.

In a seven-year follow-up statistical survey of 186 addicts treated by NET from 1973 to December 1980 (130 on drugs, 30 on alcohol, 26 on cigarettes) recently completed for the British Medical Association, it was demonstrated that 78.5 percent of those who were traced at follow-up were drug, alcohol, and cigarette-free; for drug-use only, 80 percent. The U.S. figures for other treatments show that "less than 10 percent are free of both heroin and methadone ten years after treatment."[8] Cigarettes are a harder addiction than heroin to stop, but not nearly so hard as methadone, which is the worst.

In addition, only 23 percent made alcohol a substitute dependence, and all of these temporarily. This is compared with other programs where 60 percent of the addicts treated became moderate or "heavy" drinkers. 65 percent of those who were drug and alcohol free had no "rehabilitation" at all after ten days of NET, or less than fourteen days after-treatment. The drop-out rate for all patients who began NET over the seven years was 1.6 percent. This compared with published figures in the U.S.A. and U.K. of other treatment modalities which reflected a 45 to 90 percent drop-out rate. 59 percent of the addicts treated in the clinical trials were under thirty years of age. The average length of stay in "rehabilitation" for all NET patients was sixteen days. In other programs "success" depended on the length of time in the program, usually eighteen months or longer.

2 INTRODUCTION TO ADDICTIONS

To the best of my knowledge I had never seen a drug addict until I reached Hong Kong in 1964. There, as head of surgery in an 850-bed Chinese hospital, the problems associated with drug addiction became a daily part of my professional life. I have had as many as eleven patients on some form of opiates in a ward of fourteen people; admittedly, this was an unusually high ratio, but ten to fifteen patients on narcotics in a larger ward was a regular occurrence. In 1964 the official number of opiate addicts in Hong Kong was admitted to be 100,000 in a population of under four million people. Those with experience of the drug problem said the figure was much higher.

Encounters with addiction
I had come into contact with the drug problem earlier through my journalist husband, George Patterson, who had gone to China as a missionary in 1946, right after World War II. While there, and later during three years of living and travelling in Tibet, he had seen a great deal of drug addiction—mostly opium smoking or the swallowing of opium pills.

After obtaining my Fellowship of the Royal College of Surgeons in Edinburgh, Scotland, I had gone straight to India. I taught and practiced general surgery from 1948 to 1953 at the Christian Medical College in Ludhiana, Punjab. I met George in 1952 during a holiday visit to the Indian-Tibetan border town of Kalimpong in the Himalayas of North Bengal. We were married in September 1953 during a leave in Aberdeen, Scotland.

When we returned to India in 1954—to Kalimpong where George was based while writing his articles and books, and doing lay preaching in various parts of India with indigenous Indian Christian leaders—I had no hospital in which to practice major surgery adequately. In 1956 I agreed to be superintendent of the Indian Tea Association central hospital in Darjeeling, some thirty miles from Kalimpong, with responsibility for over one hundred small outlying tea-garden hospitals. I was there for four years. For my work in building the central unit into a very effective community hospital I received a Member of the British Empire award from Her Majesty, Queen Elizabeth of England.

George and I returned to England in 1961, partly because I was eight months pregnant with our second child, and partly because George wanted to enter politics. While in London, George was unexpectedly brought into contact with the drug problem again, this time through Hephzibah Menuhin, the noted pianist, and her sociologist husband, Richard Hauser, both deeply involved with the problems of violence and drug abuse among the youth of London.

In January 1964, George left Britain to film a series of television documentaries in Asia. One of those, "Raid Into Tibet," was an account of Tibetan guerrilla activities against the Chinese occupation army inside Tibet from bases in the high Himalayas of Nepal. During this period I practiced surgery at the United Mission Hospital in Kathmandu, the capital of Nepal.

George and his television colleagues then went on to make a film about "The Opium Trail," from "the golden triangle" in northeast Burma and Thailand, to Hong Kong. I followed George to Hong Kong in September 1964 and was appointed head of surgery in the 850-bed Chinese Tung Wah Hospital, the largest hospital group in Asia.

At that time Hong Kong was said to have the world's worst drug problem. A 300-milligram packet of heroin, containing 40 percent heroin and 60 percent barbiturate, cost less than a pack of cigarettes and was as easily obtained. Almost any side alley had its drug vendor, who was prepared either to inject drugs by syringe or to sell them in powder form three times a day—or as often as wanted. The schools and colleges became riddled with drug abuse as dealers peddled their drugs like candy-sellers outside the playgrounds and playing fields.

I was aware of all this through George, who not only continued to amass information—he had been asked to write a definitive book on the drug problem by the Hong Kong Government—but who was also in demand to talk to school groups, parents, and church youth classes in addition to his professional talks on radio and television.

Encounters with acupuncture

In 1972 President Richard Nixon made his momentous visit to China, accompanied by a large entourage of journalists and doctors. The door into China which this visit opened to the West provided a fascinating variety of political opportunities and significant medical and scientific exchanges. For example, newspaper reports which flooded out of China during the presidential visit were filled with spectacular accounts of surgical operations being conducted by means of electro-acupuncture analgesia.

Shortly after his arrival in Beijing (Peking) with the presidential party, *New York Times* columnist James Reston developed appendicitis. His appendix was removed under conventional anesthesia by surgeons at the Anti-Imperial Hospital in Beijing, but afterwards he permitted an acupuncturist to apply needles to his elbow and legs to relieve post-surgical pain. Reston wrote: "There was a noticeable relaxation of pressure and distension within an hour, and no recurrence of the problem thereafter."

U.S. physicians soon began taking acupuncture seriously, especially when a group of their most eminent colleagues, including Boston heart specialist Dr. Paul Dudley White and New York ear surgeon Dr. Samuel Rosen, toured Chinese hospitals and watched fully conscious patients undergo major surgery with nothing more than acupuncture needles to anesthetize them. The operations observed by the astonished doctors included partial removal of the stomach, excision of a brain tumor, and removal of an ovarian cyst. On his return to the U.S. Dr. Rosen reported: "My colleagues and I have seen the past, and it works."

Other doctors visiting China were equally impressed by developments in Chinese medicine. Dr. E. Grey Dimond, provost of the University of Missouri Medical School in Kansas City, was one. In the *Journal of the American Medical Association* he cited advantages the Chinese had found in acupuncture anesthesia: "It is absolutely safe; there is no interruption of the patient's hydration. The patient can still receive fluid and foods. There is no post-operative nausea and vomiting. The method is convenient and readily available."

Chinese doctors told their Western colleagues they used electro-acupuncture simply because it worked. Despite its use on over 500,000 patients with a 90 percent success rate[1], they could still offer no adequate explanation of its rationale. The leading theory inside China was that acupuncture as an anesthetic involved "neuro-physiological phenomena, and that basically the twirling needles were thought to send an impulse to the brain that reduced the electrical activity there which would otherwise register pain."

I had first become interested in acupuncture in England in 1963, when my husband was assisting a senior colleague with the London *Observer,* Guy Wint, to edit a book on Asian affairs.[2] At that time Guy suffered a severe stroke which left him partially paralyzed and disordered in speech. Reduced to frustrating inactivity he also suffered continuous pain requiring heavy sedation. Guy heard of Dr. Felix Mann, a consultant in my old hospital, St. James's, Balham, who practiced acupuncture. At Guy's request I discussed the treatment with Dr. Mann. A few years later in *The Third Killer,* Guy described his experience of a variety of treatments in different parts of the world: "By far the most rewarding of these experiments was with Chinese acupuncture. It was surprising that this was so because at first the doctor who practiced it—Dr. Felix Mann from Cambridge, trained in Western medicine—asserted that it would do little for strokes, and tried to dissuade me from having this administration. Later I discovered in a Chinese handbook that the Chinese themselves use it in such cases, but they recognize that a stroke is altogether a very serious matter, and a cure is not very likely . . ."[3]

Personal experience with acupuncture

I was so impressed by Guy's improvement, and by that of several others whom I sent to Dr. Mann for treatment, that when I arrived in Hong Kong in 1964 I decided to have acupuncture treatment for my own migraine headaches. I had suffered from migraine for thirty years, with three-day attacks almost every two weeks, made tolerable only by large doses of pain-relieving drugs.

I was introduced by a mutual friend to a Chinese acupuncturist. He was a film distributor, not a doctor, but he had studied and practiced acupuncture all his life, first in China and later in France, and was well-informed on the subject of human anatomy. He recommended three courses of treatment over a period of three months.

The first month's treatments were dramatically successful. Both the frequency and intensity of the migraine attacks were reduced by 95 percent. In the second month, with the needles placed in the corner of my eye in addition to other sites, improvement was only 50 percent. In the third month, the attacks were as severe as ever and the needling, which was at first painless, became very painful.

The same acupuncturist later treated my husband very successfully for an arthritic knee stemming from damaged cartilage, the legacy of an old football injury, which began to be very painful and caused George sleepless nights. I arranged an appointment with an orthopedic surgeon colleague, who established by X-ray that there were osteoarthritic changes in the knee and gave George cortisone injections. Six weeks later the pain was back, as unbearable as ever. After two half-hour treatments with needles and electrical stimulation by the acupuncturist, however, the pain disappeared and did not return.

One of my Chinese colleagues in the Tung Wah Hospital was Dr. H. L. Wen, a well-known Hong Kong neurosurgeon who was consultant to the Neurosurgical Unit. Dr. Wen became extremely interested in the possibilities of using acupuncture anesthesia for some of his brain operations. After six weeks' visit in China to study the technique, he returned to Hong Kong and asked me, as head of surgery, to select some patients who were willing to have electro-acupuncture anesthesia for their operations instead of orthodox anesthesia. Another colleague involved in the experiments was Dr. Wen's senior assistant, Dr. Stanley Y. C. Cheung, one of my own trainee surgeons who had assisted me before sitting for his Edinburgh Fellowship and doing further advanced training at the Edinburgh Neurosurgical Unit.

Various forms of stimulation had been used by the Chinese in addition to the common needle and finger acupuncture. In injection acupuncture sterile water, saline, morphine, etc., were injected into acupuncture points. In thread acupuncture, catgut threaded to a surgical needle was passed from one acupuncture point to another. In pressure acupuncture pressure was applied to the skin over the acupuncture points.

Stimulation was achieved either manually through a push-pull or rotary movement, or by a regulatory current in the case of electro-acupuncture. Manual stimulation was carried out for ten to fifteen minutes and the needle either removed or left in place until the next session when the procedure was repeated.

Electro-acupuncture stimulation by needles gained widespread use in acupuncture anesthesia because it produced continued stimulation over longer periods of time with much less effort on the part of the operator. Also, the strength of the stimulation could be adjusted according to the needs of the patient, and a stronger stimulation could be achieved than with the manual rotation of the needles.

An unexpected discovery
Drs. Wen, Cheung and I started experimenting with the 6.26 stimulator which was widely used in China, and had a bipolar spike wave form, AC current, pulse width 0.6 msec and a frequency up to 111 hertz, or cycles per second.

While producing acupuncture analgesia by this machine, we made an unexpected discovery. In a remarkable example of serendipity (finding something valuable while searching for something else), we found that we were also curing drug addicts. Unknown to us, some of our patients had been on drugs—opium, heroin, morphine—for a number of years. Some had been heavily addicted for many years to doses far in excess of anything tolerated in the West. They volunteered the information spontaneously that within a few days after we started needling them they had, for the first time, lost their desire for drugs.

It was Dr. Wen who first suggested a possible connection between acupunctural stimulation operating on the autonomic nervous system, and the withdrawal symptoms of drug addiction. He then asked me to select a wider range of drug addicts from among the hospital patients, or from the sophisticated young addicts who, I had told him, came to our home seeking help. We began to keep a detailed record of their responses, with increasing interest.

In February 1973, a well-known American neurosurgeon and neurophysiologist, Dr. S. Irving Cooper, visited Hong Kong and gave a lecture to the Tung Wah Hospitals staff. Dr. Cooper, of St. Barnabas Hospital for Nervous Diseases in New York, became internationally known as a pioneer of several new brain operations for involuntary movement disorders (including Parkinson's Disease) and for techniques in cryogenic surgery. At his lecture Dr. Cooper revealed that he had discovered a possible means of curing spastics and epileptics by surgically implanting electrodes in the patients' brains and then stimulating them by means of a receiver implanted in the chest, activated by a pocket transmitter. His theory was that prosthetic stimulation of the cerebellum may gradually recondition reflex functioning of some brain circuits or lead to enduring neurochemical changes.[4]

These findings were deeply challenging to me. If some connection could be established between what Dr. Cooper was investigating, and our own discovery of the effects of electrically stimulated acupuncture, some tremendous possibilities might be opened up. Dr. Cooper himself was very interested when I raised the subject with him at a private meeting a few days later. He affirmed that some present theories about brain physiology might have to be reconsidered in the light of such developments. He added that recent neurosurgical evidence suggested that electrical stimulation reconditioned circuits, such as the reticular formation, so that, in conditions formerly considered incurable there was progressive improvement the longer the treatment was carried on.

Later, on reflection, an idea suddenly struck me: what if the Chinese, without knowing about electricity, had stumbled, several thousand years before, on another profound discovery? Acupuncture might well be a form of electrical stimulation to correct a metabolic imbalance; the recent electro-acupuncture stimulation might be simply eliciting a more intense form of the response than the original "twirling" practice. If so, in the drug addiction cures we had witnessed the acupuncture points would be less important than the electrical stimulation of the nerve pathways to the brain—occurring in some way yet to be identified.

To follow up these and other ideas that were emerging from our researches, I expanded my reading into the new fields of acupuncture and electrical stimulation, in Western as well as Chinese literature, to uncover any connection between electrical stimulation and drug addictions. I already knew from my own reading that Electro-Convulsive Therapy ("shock treatment") had been used in alcoholism and other addictions with marked lack of success. Somewhere between that failure and our recent successful experience with the much milder electro-acupuncture, I suspected I would find an answer.

3 "WALKING ON BOTH FEET": THE BEST OF EAST AND WEST

Chinese herbal medicine is over four thousand years old. The first pharmacy book, the *P'en T'sao,* published by the Emperor Shen Nung in 2737 B.C., listed 365 herbs as "superior, mediocre or inferior." The now famous ephedrine, brought to the notice of the West by a Dr. K. K. Chen in 1926, was listed in the *P'en T'sao* as *ma huang,* and had been used by Chinese doctors to treat asthma for four thousand years.

The *Huang Ti Nei Ching Su Wen,* or *The Yellow Emperor's Classic of Internal Medicine,* is the earliest extant medical classic of China. Written between the eighth and fifth centuries B.C., it consists of eighteen volumes covering a great variety of subjects, including the theory of diseases and their etiology, diagnosis, and treatment.

In the book, man is seen as a microcosm of the universe, subject to the same tensions as nature itself. The immutable course of nature, the *tao,* was believed to act through two opposing and unifying forces, the *yin* (negative, passive, and feminine) and the *yang* (positive, active, and masculine). In a normal person the two forces are in balance and assist the vital energy (called *chi*) to circulate to all parts of the body via a network of fourteen channels, or "meridians," each connected to an important internal organ or junction to which it branches. Obstruction (deficiency) and outpouring (excess) in the circulation of the *chi* causes an imbalance of the two forces, and thus results in disease.

Electro-Acupuncture in the East

Traditional Chinese medicine and philosophy were based on the conception of *chi*. It was believed that all things, animate or inanimate, possessed an inherent energy. This energy stabilized the chemical composition of matter, and when this matter was broken down energy was released. Water and ice have the same chemical formula, yet when ice changes into water, energy, in some form, is released. Man is made of matter, but he has life also. Thus he has two sources of energy: the electrical energy generated as a result of biochemical and biophysical changes in his cells, and the living energy inherited by his birth. Dr. Louis Moss, a Western expert on acupuncture, has stated: "It may well be that this force *(chi)* is an electrical potential emanating from the minutest cells in the body by their biochemical and biophysical exchanges."

The Chinese phrase for medicine consists of four radicals, or symbols, in two characters, one meaning a cavity with an arrow inside it, and the other meaning a knife or instrument, and alcohol. Chinese scholars interpret the phrase to mean that an arrow has created a wound and that a knife or some other instrument is needed to extract it, with alcohol applied to treat it. So, in spite of later speculations and often absurd theories as to the causation and cure of diseases, among Chinese medical practitioners a rational, semi-scientific, and dignified practice of empirical treatment has always existed, based on the accumulated knowledge of centuries and derived from acute observation by practitioners of intelligence and integrity.

Acupuncture (from the Latin *acus,* meaning "needle," and *pungere,* meaning "sting") has been used in China, some claim, for almost five thousand years in some form. But the practice of acupuncture developed in conjunction with "moxibustion," or the burning of the herb *mogwart* at or near appropriate sites of the body. Thus the Chinese name for acupuncture, *chen-chiu,* meaning "needle and heat," usually implies both practices. Acupuncture and moxibustion, combined with the use of herbs, breathing exercises, and therapeutic massage, still constitute the core of traditional Chinese medicine.

What happens in acupuncture?

The most widely accepted modern theory of how acupuncture works is that the prick of a needle at certain precisely defined points on the skin stimulates specific nerves which transmit electrical impulses via the spinal cord and lower centers of the brain, which in turn controls the affected area. Every part of the body, no matter how small, is supplied with nerves, and every millimeter of it is under the direct control of one nerve or group of nerves. Nerves control nearly all processes going on in the body. When stimulated, some nerves increase the movement of the intestines; others retard it. Some increase, other retard, the flow of digestive juices. Similarly, certain nerves can increase or decrease the rate of the heartbeat, determine the expansion or contraction of blood vessels, and so on.

Dr. Felix Mann has written: "The nervous system can be compared to the electronic control apparatus of some complex machine, like a telephone exchange or an automatic pilot. The art of acupuncture depends on knowing precisely which nerve to stimulate in a given disease. It sounds as simple as knowing which keys to press on a typewriter in order to spell your name. In fact, however, a considerable amount of knowledge is necessary before acupuncture can be practiced satisfactorily..."[1]

Before the West, with its recently developed system of scientific medicine, made an impact on China, the health of the nation depended on the practitioners of this traditional form of Chinese medicine. The Chinese doctor rarely practiced surgery and, under the Manchu dynasty, he was not allowed to do so.

With the introduction of Western medicine in China, traditional Chinese medicine in general and acupuncture in particular began to fall into disrepute as being non-scientific. In 1822, after the official "Great Imperial Board" in Peking ordered a virtual abandonment of acupuncture, Chinese intellectuals educated in Western missionary schools came to regard Chinese medicine as old-fashioned and a hindrance to the modernization and development of their country. In 1929 the Nationalist Government banned the practice of traditional Chinese medicine, including acupuncture.

Despite such official opposition, the ordinary Chinese citizen continued to believe in and use acupuncture and traditional medicine. The 80 percent of the population living in rural areas received virtually no benefit from the Western-trained doctors in the cities, and they continued to use herbal medicines and acupuncture for the relief of pain and various diseases.

Then the Communist Government, after taking office in 1949, introduced the policy of "walking on both feet," or using the best of both Chinese and Western medicine. Chairman Mao Zedong set out four concepts of health care: to serve the workers, peasants and soldiers; to put prevention first; to unite Western and traditional Chinese medicine; and to coordinate medical campaigns with mass movements. This policy gave rise to the mass medical phenomenon of "barefoot doctors," simplistically trained personnel who went into the villages, towns, and cities to treat the people.

Acupuncture anesthesia

Acupuncture was first used for surgical anesthesia in 1958. The first successful application was for tonsillectomy. Previously, following tonsillectomy under the usual local anesthesia, the patient complained of sore throat and inability to eat or drink for several days. Since acupuncture was noted to be effective in relieving sore throat and pharyngitis it was first proposed that the procedure should be used for post-operative sore throat; finally acupuncture was combined with the anesthesia procedure for the whole tonsillectomy, with great success.

The first experiments were carried out on 660 medical personnel and other volunteers, followed by 40,000 other trial cases over the next few years. From these investigations psychiatrists began to experiment with possible new methods of treatment for psychiatric diseases, on the theory that it should be possible to transmit electricity through the sensory nerves to the higher centers of the brain without adversely affecting the motor cortex, as happens in electric shock treatment.

Traditionally, psychiatric treatment aimed at inhibiting the activities of the cerebrum, with physiological as well as pathological symptoms being suppressed. When acupuncture—using the electrical stimulation—was tried, it appeared to suppress only the pathological activities, leaving the physiological activities of the cerebrum intact. In studies at the Shanghai Psychiatric Hospital, 73 percent of the patients treated showed good to fair response.[2]

One patient in a catatonic stupor lay completely motionless in bed, and did not eat, drink or utter a word. His dependence on others was total. Previously, the only treatment for this condition had been electric shock therapy, but the relapse rate was always high. After several electrical stimulations of his acupuncture points, the patient gradually recovered, not only eating and drinking normally but also talking rationally.

The investigators considered their application of electro-acupuncture through the trigeminal nerve to be analagous to the evolution of external to internal pacemakers, for heart stimulation. In order to overcome the impedance of the skin and chest wall, the external pacemaker needed a current of sixty to seventy volts and caused annoying stimulation of the chest muscles. The internal pacemaker, with the tip of the electrode in the right ventricular wall, needed a current of only one millivolt, and did not stimulate any surrounding structures.

Experiments were conducted on animals as well as humans. Sensitive electronic instruments were attached to the brain, and the electric activity of the brain recorded. Stimulation of the trigeminal nerve elicited the strongest and widest distribution of the electric waves. On the other hand, stimulation of other cranial nerves induced much weaker electric waves, of much smaller distribution.

The Chinese researchers then experimented by ignoring the acupuncture points, stimulating the areas rich in nerve endings, even the peripheral nerves, with equally satisfactory results. It was further discovered that the closer the stimulus was applied to the site of operation, the better the anesthetic effect. The results of manual stimulation, by twirling the acupuncture needle, were compared with electrical stimulation, and it was found that the anesthetic effect was almost the same.

The ear and external ear canal, which played such a key part in electro-acupuncture anesthesia, is a highly innervated area, supplied by sensory fibers of the seventh and tenth cranial nerves. The nerve endings are closely interwoven and superimposed on each other. Since these nerves have a very wide distribution the investigators theorized that stimulation of the branches in the ear had a reflex effect on practically all parts of the body.

Electrical stimulation in the West

Electrically-induced anesthesia was not new to the West, nor even introduced by China. Research for an alternative to chemical anesthesia was begun as early as 1902 in the Hospital Necker in Paris, France, where Professor Francois Leduc discovered that certain high frequency electric currents had an anesthetizing effect. By 1966 (when the first International Symposium of Electro-Anesthesia and Electro-Sleep was held in Europe) Professor Aimé Limoge, on the faculty of dental surgery at the University of Paris, had designed a high frequency generator that would keep a patient anesthetized for as long as necessary. Unlike Electro-Convulsive Therapy, where the current is of short duration and the patient remains unconscious for some time afterwards, in electrical anesthesia the patient could have a long period of current and awake immediately it was stopped.[3]

In England, in 1967, Professors P. D. Wall and W. H. Sweet reported successful treatment of eight patients with severe cutaneous pain by electrical stimulation of their peripheral nerves.[4] The following year W. H. Sweet and J. G. Wespic reported success in eighteen patients with intermittent peripheral stimulation.[5] (See Appendix I, p.159.) Then in 1974 P. D. Wall and P. W. Nathan described treating thirty patients suffering from post-herpetic neuralgia with prolonged self-administered electric stimulation from a portable apparatus. The results were good in eleven cases. In eight of these the course of the neuralgia was improved, and two were cured.[6] From their studies, Wall and Sweet produced their "gate theory" of pain control. (See Appendix II, p.159.)

Twenty years previously scientists in the Soviet Union had developed a new method of "neurotropic therapy," or electro-sleep. It had been preceded, in the U.S.S.R. and other countries in Eastern Europe, by numerous physiological studies of the effects of electric current on the animal and human brain.

Sleep therapy, based on Pavlov's concept of sleep as protective inhibition, was widely acclaimed as an important addition to therapeutic measures, comparing favorably with the disadvantages associated with drug-induced sleep. However, in spite of the acceptance of electro-sleep as a therapeutic method both in the U.S.S.R. and Europe, its widespread success in clinical practice, and extensive theoretical and experimental research (over 450 publications at that time), no uniformity of viewpoint emerged either on the mechanism of electro-sleep induction or on the mechanism of its therapeutic effect.

I was very interested in one example given by a Russian doctor, G. V. Sergeev of the Institute of Internal Medicine, U.S.S.R. Academy of Medical Sciences, Moscow, in a paper entitled "The Use of Electro-Sleep in Clinical Medicine" in which he said: "Electro-sleep, as a factor exerting a neurotropic action on the central nervous system, is used in clinical medicine for the treatment of various diseases with underlying disturbances of the cortical regulation of somatic function..."

He described his electro-sleep technique: "...rectangular pulse, constant polarity, duration of pulse 0.2–0.3 msec, current intensity 15-20 mA expressing the amplitude value of the pulse at a frequency of 80-100 pulses per sec., daily sessions lasting from 30 minutes to 2 hours, course of treatment of up to 20-25 sessions..."

Such ongoing investigations by scientists from East and West, as well as the emergence of biofeedback techniques, provided fascinating and tantalizing clues to the mystery of drug addicts being "cured" by our electro-acupuncture in Hong Kong. But one which stood out above others in my thinking was the work of Dr. W. Grey Walter, the noted neurophysiologist.[7] He was the first to correlate the frequencies of the brain's electrical waves with epileptic seizures and to describe the now well-known "alpha" and other brain rhythms associated with mood changes. (See Appendix III, p.159.)

That was the connection I needed: between electrical stimulation, brain waves (cycles per second, frequencies, hertz), and the alterations of mood — such as those induced by drugs. If I could find the coordinates of electrical frequencies and brain cycles, in much the same manner as Grey Walter had done with his epileptics, I would solve the mystery. (See Appendix IV, p.161.)

About the same time as Grey Walter was making his major advance in the understanding of epilepsy (1950), Dr. Irving Cooper was reading a book by the Italian physiologist, Giuseppe Moruzzi, who made the remarkable observation that electrical stimulation of the anterior lobe of the cerebellum could produce either an increase or decrease of decerebrate rigidity from the same point, depending on the frequency of stimulation. He found that with frequencies of 10 hertz increase of decerebrate rigidity might be activated, while frequencies of 100 to 300 hertz invariably produced a decrease. Also, the decrease of frequency of stimulation could be compensated for by increasing the duration of each stimulus. But a train of repetitive stimulation was always necessary in order to produce an inhibitory or facilitatory effect.

Twenty years later, in the winter of 1972, Dr. Cooper began implanting electrodes on the cerebellum by a surgical technique called "suboccipital craniotomy" for cases of severe epilepsy and various spastic conditions. It was these operations and findings that we discussed during his visit to Hong Kong in February 1973.

He had concluded that cerebellar stimulation arrested both the clinical seizures and the concomitant ictal EEG discharge, and that this suggested a possible cerebellar interference with electrical seizure discharge, as had already been demonstrated in animal experiments. Such a finding was in keeping with other observations of cerebellar function. For example, anterior cerebellar stimulation *did not appear clinically to affect muscular tone in normal limbs,* but did lessen tone in spastic extremities. (See Appendix V, p.163.)

Over a period of two years of such stimulation he found that there were no signs of undesirable motor, sensory, intellectual, or emotional changes.[8]

So, from the best of the West and the best of the East I had arrived at a working rationale with which to investigate the possibility of a cure for drug addictions.

4 FROM SURGERY TO RESEARCH

Over a period of three months, from January to March, 1973, we treated forty cases of drug addiction in the Tung Wah Hospital in our spare time. Thirty of these patients were opium addicts, and the other ten were heroin addicts. Six of these forty cases came voluntarily for treatment of drug addiction; the remainder for a variety of other conditions. The amount of drugs taken varied considerably among individuals, but the official average daily drug intake in Hong Kong was worth H.K. $8.6 (about U.S. $1.50). At that time this amount would buy 900 milligrams of 40–60 percent heroin mixed with 60–40 percent barbiturate.

We modified the standard acupuncture techniques of inserting needles in hand, wrist, and ears for inducing surgical analgesia by using needles in the patients' ears only. In acupuncture terminology we used the "lung" point in the middle of the concha, and here we inserted needles on each ear between the skin and the cartilage for a depth of a quarter of an inch, then connected the needles by crocodile clips and leads to the electrical stimulator. The current intensity was increased until the patient felt a slight, not unpleasant, tingling in the ear, and this was continued for an average of thirty to forty minutes per treatment, two or three treatments a day being given for five days during the acute withdrawal stage, followed by one treatment for the subsequent four or five days.

About ten to fifteen minutes after stimulation began, the patient's watering eyes and running nose became dry; the aching, shivering and abdominal pain decreased; breathing became regular, and the patient began to feel warm and relaxed.

Dr. Wen and Dr. Cheung reported the results in *The Asian Journal of Medicine:*

"Of the 40 cases, 39 were discharged and are free of drug addiction (one was discharged to another hospital for surgery of tumor of the bladder). These patients have gained weight and said that they have since had no urge to take the drug. Twenty-two of these cases had their urine sent for investigation to see if it was positive for drugs. The report showed one doubtful case, and one positive case... The 'doubtful' result related to a case of concussion, who had been put on Luminal for post-concussional syndrome. The one positive case was suffering from tumor of the bladder, which necessitated injections of narcotic to stop his pain. The 20 cases which showed negative urine tests are free of the drug and so far have no urge for it either... Up to the present, eight cases have come back to have one or two repetitions of treatment...Each of them was given the treatment as an out-patient, and so far they have no recurrence of the symptoms..."[1]

Over the next four months we treated more than one-hundred cases of heroin and opium addiction, with similar results. (See Appendix VI, p.164.)

New hope for addicts

The successful treatment of these patients, with others I was treating privately in Hong Kong, opened up new hope for possible cures of hitherto intractable conditions. In so many ways Hong Kong was the ideal place in which to conduct such research, with its fine hospitals and a huge drug problem. Yet the official attitude towards the drug problem was almost paranoid. Because of political, social, and financial factors Hong Kong authorities seemed more concerned with concealing the scale of the problem than with finding a possible medical solution.

Pressure was applied to Dr. Wen, Dr. Cheung, and myself to stop all experiments with acupuncture anesthesia, but because acupuncture, as a traditional Chinese form of medicine, was allowed by law to be practiced in Hong Kong, it could not be stopped legally. Strongly worded circulars issued by official medical authorities threatened us with severe consequences; there were warnings against our giving public lectures (after Dr. Wen had given one to a packed audience of doctors). There was also pressure through the hospital (where we were conducting our research in addition to our own surgical responsibilities), and official denials to the local and international press that anything medically significant in the area of drug addiction cure had happened, although several reports had already appeared in the *New York Times* and the London *Observer.*

Our research and the reports in the media had emphasized the use of acupuncture, mainly because of the widespread interest following on James Reston's article, and the subsequent articles by doctors accompanying President Nixon. But I was increasingly convinced from my reading and personal observations that acupuncture was not the key to the success of the treatment. Rather, some unknown electrical factor associated with frequencies was producing the results. From my own Chinese medical colleagues who knew a great deal about the history and practice of traditional acupuncture I knew that it was not effective in treating drug addictions, although it did help with muscle relaxation.

But if I wanted to test my thesis, and satisfy my mounting interest in the medical and scientific potential of electrical stimulation, I would not only have to leave Hong Kong to pursue the research but I would also have to give up the surgery which I had loved and practiced for so long. Was our recent discovery important enough for me to do this?

From my reading and widening clinical experience I had become increasingly convinced that it was electrical stimulation of nerve pathways, rather than the system of electro-acupuncture, which was the important factor in the addictive curative process.

For example, when experimenting with the electrical current by varying the frequencies and wave forms, I found that certain frequencies were dramatically effective while with other patients the same frequencies were woefully inadequate. Chinese addicts given a treatment of 111 hertz on the Chinese model 6.26 stimulator would respond positively, describing the sensation as being like an average shot of heroin. Yet treatment at that frequency had little or no effect on amphetamine addicts.

I resolved, therefore, to design my own machine with a much wider range of frequencies and wave-forms, and have it built to my own specifications, which would allow me to experiment. I was now receiving reports of exciting developments from researchers investigating electrical stimulation in other countries, which increased my interest even more.

Inside China, the Kuang-si Medical College Group published a report of investigations carried out on fifty-two normal animals, in the *Scientia Sinica*. The anesthetic effect of acupuncture was compared before and after the administration of a variety of drugs affecting the nervous system, and it was found that some increased the effectiveness of acupuncture anesthesia whereas others invariably reduced it. (See Appendix VII, p. 164.)

Another group of Chinese researchers in Peking Medical College filmed a series of experiments with rabbits,[2] which I saw when it was shown in Hong Kong. They studied the parts played by various brain chemicals in acupuncture analgesia and especially the effects of substances that were known to be involved in the transmission of nerve impulses and thus were probably concerned in both pain and analgesia.

The film showed two rabbits with their circulations linked. Only one received acupuncture to induce analgesia, yet the pain threshold was raised significantly in *both* animals. In another experiment, cerebro-spinal fluid from one acupunctured rabbit was transferred to a non-acupunctured rabbit. The pain threshold of the second rabbit was considerably increased though not as greatly as in the first rabbit.

Acupuncture by finger pressure was used on the rabbits rather than the widely-known needles, since needles caused too much local tissue damage. Some Chinese claim that historically finger acupuncture was probably the first method used, and it was coming back into favor. This film gave me the first indication that needles might not be necessary—that surface electrodes could be used.

Later reports in the West confirmed the importance of these observations. The *London Times* Science Report of March 28, 1974, declared: "As well as providing valuable and interesting evidence that the mechanism of acupuncture analgesia is different from that mediated by morphine, the parallel experiments run with morphine show that the methods of investigation and measurement that the authors are pursuing are valid, and that the conclusions they draw are to be considered seriously. There seems little doubt that acupuncture produces changes that result in the blocking of pain impulses in the brain..."[3]

Researchers in the West were also finding in their rat and cat experiments that when animals were stimulated through electrodes placed in the periaqueductal grey, they "become totally unresponsive to pain while retaining a normal ability to respond to other stimuli and that the effect outlasted the stimulation by several hours."[4] (See Appendix VIII, p. 165.)

I had kept in touch with Dr. Cooper by correspondence, and he told me of treating a patient with severe action myoclonus of three years' duration, a sequel of cerebral anoxia. For the first few weeks after implantation and stimulation at 200 hertz there was no improvement, but improvement did come gradually, so that within a few months of continuous stimulation her totally incapacitating generalized twitching had virtually disappeared. He had also treated about thirty other patients suffering from hypertonic states such as cerebral palsy, the consequences of stroke, and various forms of spastic paralysis as well as intractable epilepsy, with dramatic success. The technique he used was to implant electrodes in the brain by surgery, and to control stimulation of the cerebellum by what he termed "the prosthetic mobilization of the inhibitory potential of the cerebellar cortex" (that is, making use of hitherto untapped functions of the cerebellum by means of electrical stimulation).

"The cerebellum is an inhibitory mechanism functioning somewhat as a rheostat," Dr. Cooper explained. "It has a modulating function on the rest of the brain. The evidence for its function has built up over the years in animal experiments. What is new is the application of some of this knowledge to human disease."

Dr. Cooper devised the "Cooper Brain Pacemaker" to cure neural disorders. Plates of silicone-coated Dacron mesh, to which were attached four or eight pairs of platinum disc electrodes were surgically placed on the patients' cerebellar cortex. (See Appendix IX, p.165.)

The electrode plates were connected with subcutaneous leads to a small radio frequency receiver that was implanted in the patient's chest before brain surgery began. Electrode stimulation originated from a transmitter carried outside the body, and occurred by trans-epidermal inductive coupling by means of an antenna taped to the patient's chest directly over the receiver. The transmitter, about the size of a pack of cigarettes, could be carried in a pocket or purse.

Dr. Cooper doubted that the natural course of cerebral palsy, or of the other diseases he was treating, would be changed by cerebellar stimulation. However, he did feel that "*prosthetic stimulation of the cerebellum may gradually recondition reflex functioning of some brain circuits.*"

He had observed behavioral changes in all his patients, even in the few who had had little or no physical improvement. All of his patients were independently evaluated before and after surgery and in continued follow-up, and exhibited the following behavioral changes: (1) reduced tension, anxiety, and feeling of stress; (2) improved rationality and fluency of speech; (3) reduced depression, and increased optimism; (4) reduced feelings of anger and of aggressive outbursts associated either with seizures or between seizures, and improved emotional control.[5]

A scientific jigsaw puzzle

The many pieces of the scientific jigsaw puzzle portraying electrical stimulation were beginning to fit together. A strong connection *had already been made* between electrical stimulation and pain, emotion and altered states of consciousness. A connection *appeared highly probable* between electrical stimulation and drugs of addiction, with their altered emotions and states of consciousness.

I read of a series of "Skinner box" experiments investigating causes of drug dependence in rats. A stimulating electrode was permanently implanted in the medial forebrain bundle of the brain, so that this bundle of neurons was stimulated whenever the rat pressed a lever. This indicated noradrenalin as the main mediator of reward. (See Appendix X, p. 166.)

Such experiments supported the theory that drugs of dependence induced euphoria by enhancing production of noradrenalin (and related catecholamines) in the brain.

The important question for me was whether electrical stimulation produced the same results in humans.

Dr. H. O. J. Collier, a British scientist, described the significance of the "Skinner box" experiments in drug dependence:

"In animals whose psychic processes are observable through their behavior we may speak of 'behavioral dependence' which may include psychic and physical components... An animal is usually prepared in dependence studies with an intravenous cannula connected to an infusion pump, which is activated by a lever in the wall of the cage. By pressing the lever the animal can self-inject drugs... If the animal is offered a strong instead of a weak solution of heroin the pattern of its lever-pressing will be different. It will learn to press the lever more and more often.

"An analogy can be drawn between self-injection of a rewarding drug and the behavior seen when the animal is prepared so that it can stimulate electrically a certain point in its own brain... In this situation a rat usually stimulates its brain several times an hour... In the most general terms, a multiplication induced by the drug of dependence of some kind of receptor or enzyme, carrier, neurone, or storage site that handles, or reacts to, an active endogenous substance mediating or modulating neuronal responses, appears to be nearest to explaining dependence. . ."[6]

In March 1973, Dr. Solomon Snyder and researcher Candace Pert of the Johns Hopkins University School of Medicine in Baltimore, reported in *Science* that they had succeeded in locating in the brain the receptor sites that attracted opioids.[7] The area of the brain with the heaviest concentration of opioid receptors was the *corpus striatum*, which seems to play a part in integrating motor activity and perceptual information. The receptors occurred much less frequently in the cerebral cortex, which regulates higher intellectual functions, and in the brain stem, which controls sleeping and wakefulness.

Snyder concluded that the ideal opioid agonist should be potent, long-lasting, non-addictive, orally administered and free from side-effects. When given over a period of time to an ex-addict such a substance would, he hoped, decondition heroin-seeking behavior and possibly result in psychological changes as well.

I wondered if such a hope were to be found, not only in some chemical substance, but in electrical stimulation? From the beginning of experimentation the idea had been implicit that the use of electricity for stimulation could produce physiological activity. There was every reason, therefore, for the idea of stimulation to be introduced in current medical thinking, even though the results of such stimulation differed from normal physiological responses.

A leading article in *The Lancet*, discussing the "sheer technical trickery" of using an implanted electrode to determine normal functioning in an individual, concluded:

"There seems to be no reason why not. When Delgado, using such stimulation, stopped a charging bull at a gallop, what was arresting was not only the bull's deceleration, but also the fact that the bull's rage was turned off. . . It looked as though a true physiological effect had been produced on the animal's behavior. This limbic lobe, which has taken over automatic and emotional or temperamental functions, acts in a simple on-off way over a long time scale, and seems eminently suitable for true stimulation. Although many parts of it have been stimulated, our knowledge of the possibilities of long-term stimulation has hardly begun, despite the fact that Delgado and co-workers have made many investigations on animals, including primates, and even a few human beings. . ."[8]

The same *Lancet* lead article described a case of spontaneous pain aris- ing from a "predominantly cortical" lesion which was relieved by intermit- tent electrical stimulation through an electrode stereotactically implanted in or near the internal capsule:

"The temporal cortex, as in all reported cases of this sort, was known to be damaged and the patient showed loss of right-parietal activity—that is, of functions on the left side of the body. The stimulating electrode was reckoned to be in the posterior limb of the internal capsule. Bipolar stimu- lation with waves of 0.25 msecs, 100 to 150 per second, 1.5 to 2.5 volts, pro- duced a sensation of light tingling and vibration. After five to fifteen minutes, pain and an unpleasant spreading dysaesthesia disappeared, to remain at bay for one to twenty-six hours. *The exact form of the electrical current is important.* With these characteristics and the symptoms experi- enced by the patient it is likely that true stimulation was produced . . ." (my italics)

Structural changes

Earlier experiments in England by Dr. L. S. Illis of Southampton, England, had also demonstrated possible structural changes after electrical stimula- tion. (See Appendix XI, p. 166.) I wrote to him regarding his experiments with electrical stimulation, describing some of my own experience. He re- plied: "I was particularly interested in your comments about the possibility of electrical stimulation altering tissue growth. I thought you might be in- terested in some work showing the effect of repetitive stimulation on the central nervous system. Since publishing that paper I have come across two further reports of similar experiments, with similar results—re a struc- tural change after stimulation."

Dr. Robert Becker, Professor of Orthopedic Surgery at the Upstate Medi- cal Center, New York State, and Medical Investigator at the Veteran's Ad- ministration Hospital, Syracuse, New York, was a leading international authority on electrical stimulation as well as an expert on the subject of tis- sue regeneration. Having succeeded in stimulating regeneration in labora- tory animals, Dr. Becker had begun to apply his technique to humans for fractured bones showing non-union.

Becker's work in tissue regeneration dated back to 1958 when he and his colleagues began experiments to determine whether electrical stimulation could trigger bone and other tissue growth in animals. Earlier research had already established that the chances of regeneration in a species depended on the proportion of nerve tissue in the areas of regeneration. Becker pointed out the inability of man, with roughly 70 percent of his total nerve mass concentrated in his brain, to regenerate, whereas salamanders, with half the mass of their nerve tissue in their brains and the remainder distributed throughout their bodies, can grow new tails, legs, and even heart tissue. Becker theorized that he could increase the regenerative powers of higher animals, somehow compensating for the small proportion of nerve tissue in their extremities, by bolstering the electrical activity in the nerve network. After amputating limbs from thirty-nine rats he planted electrodes in the amputation sites and applied current to stimulate cell changes. All but two of the rats responded with some limb growth; many regenerated amputated forelegs as far as the first joint.[9]

At a Symposium on Bioelectrochemistry in France, Becker further expanded his theories to postulate "a complete operational system existing in living organisms which controls such basic functions as growth, healing and biological cycles." He described the system as "a data transmission system in an analog fashion using varying levels of direct current as its signal. The system interlocks physically with the nervous system and is postulated to be its precursor." The direct current system is linked to the nervous system, and to all body cells. "The concept explains the biological effects of applied electrical currents including: *electrical anesthesia, electrical growth control and electro-acupuncture.* It also furnishes a testable hypothesis for predicting other effects that might be of clinical significance."[10] (my italics) (See Appendix XII, p. 167.)

A difficult decision

Although I now felt that I had enough information for a working hypothesis and a possible rationale for electrical stimulation as a successful treatment for chemical substance addiction, I was in a more difficult situation than either Dr. Cooper or Dr. Becker. Dr. Cooper was a neurosurgeon attached to a training hospital and Dr. Becker was an orthopedic surgeon attached to a research laboratory. Whereas both were well-known in the United States, as well as world-wide, I was a general surgeon who had spent the past twenty-five years doing all kinds of surgery in sometimes primitive conditions in Asia and was unknown in the field of addictions.

But after nine months of treating over one hundred Hong Kong addicts by electro-acupuncture with dramatic effect, and reading widely of the growing importance of the electrical stimulation of nerve pathways, I was faced with the difficult choice of either abandoning my surgery or giving up a medical possibility which far exceeded my surgery in importance.

I decided to leave surgery and return to London to pursue my research into what I was already calling "NeuroElectric Therapy," or NET for short.

5 INITIAL DEVELOPMENT OF NET

Most of my time after returning to England in 1973 was devoted to reviewing the material written on electrical stimulation of various kinds in different countries, and to developing my own NeuroElectric stimulator. As soon as we had moved into a home and consulting room in Harley Street, London's medical Mecca, I applied for a research grant from the official Medical Research Council. They were interested and sympathetic, but refused my application. (A highly-placed friend told me later that the psychiatrists on the committee had strongly objected to my application on the grounds that I was a surgeon rather than a psychiatrist, and hence inadequately prepared to pursue research into the treatment of addictions.) However, the Council officially encouraged me to pursue my investigations in my spare time.

First stages of my research in England

The personal interest and cooperation of several friends and patients enabled me to continue with my research. Violinist Yehudi Menuhin, for example, introduced me to his friend, Andrew Grima, jeweller to the Queen, who worked with me for several months to design a suitable ear-clip incorporating a needle so tiny that it caused no pain. (I had found that my European patients could not tolerate the pain of the Chinese acupuncture needles in their ears.)

Another friend of Yehudi Menuhin, David Shackman of Shackman Instruments Limited, put all his firm's facilities at my disposal. His managing director, Geoff Bennett, patiently worked with me to produce a stimulator built to my specifications. I had tried the only stimulators available in Britain at that time (all imported from the United States) and found them useless for my purposes. But Geoff Bennet knew nothing of biology, naturally; and I knew nothing of electronics.

Historical antecedents
From my reading I had learned that electro-physiology as a term and as a science originated in the sixteenth century. At about the same time that Galileo was inventing the compound telescope and establishing a new cosmology, an English physician, William Gilbert, was combining his practice of medicine with investigations of magnetism and "electricity" — a word coined by Gilbert. He also invented the first instrument for measuring electric fields, the electroscope.

In the early seventeenth century Francis Bacon laid the philosophical foundations of science, and in 1628 William Harvey described for the first time how blood circulates in the human body. In the same century Descartes presented his view of the biological concepts of structure, function, and mind within a framework of mathematical physics at a time when scientific societies were springing up all over Europe.

The eighteenth century brought an upsurge of interest in electricity, and Stephen Hales, one of several clergymen with an interest in science, suggested that nerves functioned by conducting "electrical powers." The Abbe´ Nolet tried to cure paralysis by electricity, and Abraham Bennet invented a "gold-leaf electroscope" for detecting and measuring electric charges.

In 1775, Luigi Galvani in Italy began his experiments in electricity and biology, and the first of a series of extraordinary "accidents" occurred. In 1786 one of Galvani's assistants, while dissecting a frog's legs, happened to touch the nerve to the muscles with his scalpel while a static electrical machine was operating on a table nearby. This made the muscle contract, thereby launching a period of major advances in the understanding of electricity and biology. Before the end of the century Galvani's nephew,

Giovanni Aldini, a physicist, reported treating a patient suffering from a personality disorder by administering currents to the head. The patient's personality steadily improved and eventually he was completely healed.

In Copenhagen, Denmark, Hans Christian Oersted noticed, while giving a lecture, that every time he produced an electrical current the needle of a demonstration compass lying on the table moved. From that chance observation he developed a series of experiments to demonstrate electromagnetism.

In the nineteenth century Carlo Matteucci, an Italian professor of physics, proved beyond doubt that an electrical current was generated by injured tissues. An experimenter in Berlin working for Johannes Muller, the world's foremost physiologist at that time, duplicated Matteucci's experiment, and went beyond it. He discovered that when a nerve was stimulated, a measurable electrical impulse was produced at the site of stimulation and travelled at high speed down the nerve, causing the muscle to contract.

In the twentieth century, the interest of two American doctors already mentioned, Cooper and Becker, in the work of Matteucci and other Italian scientists led to the development of their work in cerebellar and bone electrical stimulation.

As in earlier centuries, "accidental" discoveries played a role in the advance of scientific knowledge. Cooper, described as "the father of cryogenic surgery," conceived of that technique while opening a bottle of wine with a carbon-dioxide bottle-opener. In 1967, Becker described how while studying the electrical factors associated with fracture healing, "a regenerative-type growth process in the frog was inadvertently discovered by our group."[1] And of course our discovery that electro-acupuncture "cured" addictions was made while we were experimenting with analgesia, an entirely different field.

My own research continues

During the years 1973 to 1975 Geoff Bennett and I developed two machines which gave me an increasing number of accurate responses based on my working hypothesis, but it was very hit or miss. It was more hit than miss, however, with enough hits to convince me that my hypotheses and researches in the exciting new field of bioengineering were a possible major step toward a cure for the scourge of addictions.

The second "Shackman-Patterson" machine which we developed had a variety of wave-forms, pulse widths from 0.1 to 1.5 msecs, and frequencies varying from 5 to 2000 hertz. This transistorized machine included both the standard square or rectangular wave form used in most bio-electric treatments and in intracranial implantations, and the spike form used by the Chinese. They, presumably—although it is not stated in any publication available outside China—had some special reason for using this particular form. Our machine could also insert a modulation of 50 KHz (I discovered later that French researchers were inserting a 100 KHz modulated signal in their electro-anesthesia machine).[2]

In the first six months of research, from November 1973 to June 1974, I concluded that twirling of the acupuncture needle produced a mild electrical current, thereby altering the electrical phenomena occurring in every nerve cell. Clinical evidence indicated that NET might be producing regeneration of neurons, or, at least, a reconditioning of some brain circuits, such as the reticular formation.

I discussed those ideas with Professor Patrick Wall, one of the formulators of the "gate theory" of pain. Wall was reluctant to accept the possibility that I could be regenerating brain tissue. Yet, he said, it seemed clear that I was affecting the brain circuits in some specific way.

In my opinion, this could only be due to some chemical being released by brain cells because of the constant delay of ten to fifteen minutes before an addict starting NET experienced any relief of withdrawal symptoms. Moreover, the patients I was treating were also undergoing psychological changes for the better. For convenience, I referred to that hypothetical substance as "Chemical X."

Although I did not know the nature of "Chemical X," I was encouraged by the continued success in my clinical experience with patients and their rapid and consistent response to the electrical stimulation. After all, most effective medical treatments had emerged in this way, accidentally, and without prior scientific validation. Penicillin was saving lives long before biologists unravelled the precise molecular secrets of how bacteria caused disease.

Chemical breakthrough
In 1975—one month after the first "Interim Report" of my work was published in England—another scientific breakthrough was announced, which has since been acclaimed as one of the great discoveries of the cen-

tury. In Aberdeen University, Scotland, Dr. Hans Kosterlitz and Dr. John Hughes discovered the presence of a natural substance, enkephalin, in the medial brainstem of rats.[3]

Almost simultaneously their findings were confirmed in Sweden and in the United States by other researchers.[4,5] Following the discovery of enkephalin several other naturally occurring substances were discovered and identified and given the generic name of "endorphins" (from "endogenous morphine"). The endorphins were substances normally present in the body that acted like morphine. One of them, β-endorphin, or beta-endorphin, was demonstrated by Smyth in the Institute of Neurology, London, to be up to two hundred times more potent in pain-killing effect than morphine.[6]

Research papers on the endorphins began to appear in a variety of scientific journals as other scientists expanded this major field of investigation. β-endorphin belonged to a class of neuropeptides, many of which are found in areas of the brain known to be involved in the physiology of pain and emotions, and may be related to some biochemical mechanism involved in mental illness through alterations in the homeostatic regulation of the naturally occurring substances.[7]

Addiction to opioid drugs like morphine and heroin was assumed by Kosterlitz and Hughes to be the result of some interaction between the natural and synthetic opioid pain-killers. The opioid abstinence syndrome (commonly known as "withdrawal") can be precipitated within a few minutes by an injection of the drug naloxone. It was soon realized that the analgesic and other "behavioral and physiological effects of the endorphins" were immediately reversed by naloxone injection. This finding has continued to be a useful tool in identifying endorphin activity in research procedures. These endogenous substances were thought to act as neurotransmitters or neuromodulators at synaptic junctions of neurons, but unlike morphine they are very rapidly destroyed in the brain by enzymes.[8]

One of the unsatisfactory features of prolonged administration of the endorphins, natural or synthetic, is that they induce tolerance and dependency just as other opioids do and cross-tolerance develops between morphine and endorphins. This has diminished earlier hopes that the discovery of endorphins would lead to the synthesis of pain-killing drugs that would produce neither tolerance nor dependency.

On the other hand, the discovery of endorphins increased the potential of my NeuroElectric stimulation immensely. Dr. Kosterlitz had been my tutor at Aberdeen University so I arranged to meet him to talk about my own research findings. He was tremendously interested and made a number of helpful suggestions. He also told me of other scientists who were working with electrical stimulation and enkephalin, and agreed that my "Chemical X" was possibly enkephalin.

My theory was that by competing for the opioid receptors in the brain, synthetic opioids led to a gradual decrease in production of the natural enkephalins. Hence, a person using opioids regularly needed an increasing dose of synthetic opioids to make good the loss, creating the condition of tolerance. This diminishing of the body's natural opioids and the consequent need to ingest more synthetic opioids created the typical "drug hunger" of the addict, and the "craving" or withdrawal symptoms when the synthetic drug was withheld.

According to Kosterlitz and Hughes, a consistently maintained dosage of morphine stopped the release of enkephalin from the neurons through some feed-back mechanism. This new theory concerning the mechanism of the addiction process explained the brain's dependency on morphine as a substitute for its own naturally occurring pain-killer enkephalin.[9]

I could now see a possible link between Kosterlitz and Hughes' feed-back mechanism, Becker's "hybrid data transmission and control system," and Melzack's "central biasing mechanism," influencing transmission at all synapses.[10]

Concurrent research into "Stimulation-Produced Analgesia (SPA)" achieved by implanting electrodes in the brains of animals or humans, and its relationship to the effects on neurotransmitters, elucidated some of my clinical observations in patients undergoing NeuroElectric Therapy (NET), as my own treatment was now called. I had noted that when certain drugs, including narcotics and cocaine, were ingested or injected during a course of NET, the anticipated physical and psychic effects of these drugs were diminished, and occasionally a patient would even experience a very severe aversive effect.

The literature revealed that very powerful analgesia could be produced in rats,[11] cats[12] and monkeys[13] by electrical stimulation of certain areas of the brain, particularly the periaqueductal grey area.[14] Significantly, although such stimulation made an animal totally unresponsive to pain, it retained a normal ability to respond to other stimuli.[15] That contrasted with the effects of drugs used clinically for analgesia or narcosis.[16] Nor did stimulation reduce alertness or elicit seizures[17,18]. Further, it was stimulation and not destruction of the cells which produced the analgesia; actual electrolytic lesions produced different and harmful effects.[19,20,21] (See Appendix XIII, p.168.)

Dr. J. C. Liebeskind, well-known for his work in electrical stimulation, declared the importance of the hypotheses, supported by a considerable amount of evidence, that "electrical stimulation releases enkephalin or in some other way makes it available for binding at opiate receptor sites, whereas morphine, by resembling the natural substance, interacts with these receptors directly."[22]

Another interesting development in the investigations of the interactions between Stimulation-Produced Analgesia and enkephalin was that the antagonist naloxone reversed the effects of both[23,24] though not completely in the case of SPA.[25] This was demonstrated in a man whose severe pain was completely controlled through a stereotactically implanted electrode, but who developed acute pain when naloxone was injected and none when a placebo (saline) was injected.[26] The effect was unlikely to have been induced by suggestion, because hypnosis-induced analgesia is not modified by naloxone.[27] Thus, electrical stimulation could obviously control pain without the undesirable effects of drugs usually used for pain.

Excitement in scientific circles ran high over such results. But some researchers felt a need to dampen popular hopes for an immediate cure for addictions, arguing that there was no hope of developing an analgesic peptide with a lessened risk of dependence liability. They saw hope only in developing drugs "that act indirectly either to activate the enkephalin system or to cause the direct release of enkephalin."[28]

That was exactly what I was doing with electrical stimulation. Since NET apparently carried with it no dependence liability, I was more hopeful of a possible cure for addictions than many of my more cautious colleagues. Further, to implant electrodes in the brains of drug dependents, or even hardened drug addicts, for stimulation purposes seemed to me to be an unwarranted physical interference. I was already using external stimulation to do the same thing more effectively.

What I now had to find was the most effective external means of delivering the appropriate electrical stimulus to trigger the release of enkephalin. In animals, external electrical stimulation was as effective in altering the activity of opioid receptors as direct stimulation seemed to be.[29] One researcher estimated that 45 percent of the current applied externally in electro-sleep (where the electrodes were applied fronto-occipital, or frontomastoid) passed through the brain, and that an applied current of only one milliampere was sufficient to modify spontaneous firing of neurons.[30] However, Becker and I thought that 45 percent was an overestimation.

The discovery of enkephalin was only the beginning of a whole new branch of science. The finding that the body has receptors to which its own natural opioids attach led to the idea that the body has other receptors to which other chemical substances attach,[31,32] opening up a whole new world of natural substances, systems, and effects.

That idea was a further stimulus to me. I was finding in treating patients that for each of the different substances of addiction—opioids, alcohol, nicotine, barbiturates, cocaine, marijuana, amphetamines, tranquilizers—a specific electrical frequency was needed to treat that particular addiction. Those addicted to narcotics because of severe, chronic pain presented yet another problem to be solved. There was no point in detoxifying them from their pain-killers unless NET could also relieve or reduce their pain.

6 THE IMPORTANCE OF FREQUENCIES

Fifteen months of clinical observations convinced me that the ear-clip I had designed with the tiny needle was as unnecessary as acupuncture needles. Because the electrical stimulus could be transmitted adequately through the skin without needles,[1] I designed a blunt electrode on an ear-clip to be applied to the same area of the concha of the ear. This had the added advantages of eliminating the pain of needling and the risks of local infection or hepatitis transmitted through unsterile needles.[2]

Finding the right frequencies

My "Shackman-Patterson" neuro-stimulator[3] incorporated the most important factors in treating substance addictions: (1) greater varieties in wave-forms (e.g., in insomnia); (2) pulse-width (e.g., in pain control); (3) frequencies to match different types of drugs (e.g., the stimulant amphetamine group or the depressant opioid group), or the more difficult combination of drugs (e.g., heroin and cocaine), or psychologically associated conditions such as depression and anxiety.

From the surprisingly extensive literature on bioelectricity, I decided that the useful range of frequencies lay within the 1 hertz to 2,000 hertz range which is well clear of the diathermy range beginning at 5,000 hertz or higher. The optimum pulse widths appeared to be between 0.1 and 1.5 milliseconds.

The hoop-shaped blunt electrodes of stainless steel (conducting area 2.5 millimeters in diameter) were attached to the ear by the clip's tension, with electrode jelly applied to improve conduction. They were held in place by a headset worn either on top of the head, or around the neck, whichever was more comfortable. Patients experienced only a slight and not unpleasant tingling sensation on the skin.

The only adverse side-effects observed in the early years of testing were occasional agitation at the higher frequencies; or, on a few occasions, nausea and headache. But these symptoms were easily reversed by further treatment at a lower frequency, and a reduced current intensity. For some reason still not clear to me the polarity of the current was significant; the patients who claimed better results when the polarity was reversed were all, interestingly, left-handed.

From the start of NET treatment I gave no drugs of any kind. The drugs of addiction were completely discontinued and no replacement methadone, tranquilizers or sedatives were given. For any patient who had also been using barbiturates I withdrew the barbiturates gradually, because at that time I had not established which frequencies could be relied on to prevent withdrawal convulsions. However, two heavily addicted patients stopped all their barbiturates without reporting it to me, and yet had no convulsions. Both had previously experienced severe withdrawal convulsions when unable to obtain their usual dose of barbiturates.

It was in Hong Kong that we had the first clinical indication of the mood-altering qualities of varying frequencies. When we changed the frequency from 111 hertz to 250 hertz the Chinese addicts almost immediately reported a sensation of euphoria. The next such observation was in London when an out-patient addict came off his methadone easily after four two-hour sessions, but his addiction to intravenous Ritalin (methylphenidate hydrochloride, an amphetamine-like drug) was undiminished. I had just received the prototype of my stimulator with a higher range of frequencies, and the first treatment I gave to this patient at 2,000 hertz (a frequency chosen as an educated guess) totally relieved his craving for Ritalin for eighteen hours.

The *Lancet*, discussing the place of intuition and imagination in scientific advances, has stated: "Many discoveries fundamental to modern science have been the result of a mental flash. Meanwhile, science is retrospective; it proves the educated guess..."[4]

Another series of "happy accidents" opened up a whole new range of treatment applications. Because certain patients have already talked openly and often to the media about the beneficial effects of their NET treatment, I can use actual names here without violating medical confidentiality.

Musical frequencies help NET

Early on in my research, a close friend asked me if I would treat the British rock music star, Eric Clapton (in the 60s and early 70s huge placards at rock concerts declared "Clapton is God"), who was badly incapacitated because of heroin addiction. Known internationally as the greatest blues guitarist of his time, his ability to play or compose had virtually disappeared as his addiction had increased. At the time I was still using the first model of my stimulator, and acupuncture needles, with intermittent treatments, but within five weeks Eric was off all drugs. Within three months he was back on the world's stage "playing better than ever before" according to music critics.

Eric's willingness to talk about his heroin addiction, and his cure by NET, led to dramatic developments. First, two international record companies, The Robert Stigwood Organization and Atlantic Records, began to fund my research; and second, other rock musicians began to come to me for treatment. The funding was very important to keep the research going, but I also gained vitally important technical information from my rock musician patients. Many of them were experts in acoustic music, electronic synthesizers and the effects of amplification, which meant that they knew a great deal about frequencies and their effects on people's minds and moods.

They were also fascinated to think that their knowledge, combined with mine, could help them free themselves and others from their addictions, so they spent hours experimenting with my NET machine at different frequencies of their own choosing to test and prove the effects on themselves. They confirmed my own impressions that to obtain optimum effects, the pulse frequency had to be changed several times a day, presumably in order to respond to physiological and psychological changes in the course of the treatment.

One musician had used LSD while he was performing before an audience of 52,000 in the United States. He noticed that he could affect himself subjectively and his audience objectively by changing the types of music he played. When he played music with a certain rhythm and tempo he subjectively experienced the audience in colors of black and yellow and red, like a flaming fire; when he changed the music and tempo, he "saw" the audience as white and blue and felt serenely calm. The audience reacted correspondingly. He had analyzed the types of music which produced those effects, and was convinced that it was the frequencies which were significant.

Whenever we hit the right frequencies to "match" whatever drugs they were addicted to, the musicians would say, "it just *feels* right." If the frequency they chose differed from my choice of frequency, invariably theirs had the best and most immediate effect. Later, this was to be dramatically confirmed in my laboratory work with rats.[5,6]

I tried the same method for my own very severe and frequent migraine headaches, going through the whole range of frequencies until I found one that felt "right." This reduced my migraines to negligible mildness and infrequent occurrence. In treating my migraines I also discovered that the pain eased most when I turned up the voltage sufficiently to cause my occipital muscles to go into clonic spasm—not, by the way, a painful procedure. One hashish addict, in her second treatment, turned up the voltage until most of her scalp muscles were contracting strongly. Afterwards, she told me she felt as if her "brain had been cleansed."

In Hong Kong, when we treated heroin and opium addicts who were showing acute withdrawal symptoms, we noticed that the signs of withdrawal began to diminish about ten to fifteen minutes after beginning treatment. In another five or ten minutes some patients even fell asleep. In a total of thirty minutes or so all were comfortable and happy. We therefore set thirty minutes as a recommended time for any one treatment; but in London, I increased that to a basic forty minutes for out-patient treatment.

I encouraged in-patients, both alcohol and drug addicts, to keep the machine on continuously if possible. By the time I had developed my third stimulator model, I found that ten days was enough to treat almost all patients on *any* drug of addiction, no matter how long they had used the drug, nor how large the daily dosage. Occasionally the ten days had to be extended when there were complications either because of the condition of the patient or because of the drug combinations used.

None of the earlier patients treated in Hong Kong or London received any structured rehabilitation. Despite the good results obtained, I was convinced the treatment would be even more effective if combined with supportive rehabilitation. The rehabilitative process in association with NET would have to begin on the second or third day because the addicts became responsive to counseling with unusual rapidity.

This rapid return to alertness and responsiveness is one of the most impressive features of NET, contrasting strongly with the lethargy and depression which accompanies all other forms of treatment.[7,8,9,10,11] Friends and relatives often commented on how rapidly a patient was returning to the kind of person he or she was before going on drugs.

The BBC-TV films on NET

For a film made for television by the British Broadcasting Corporation, I was asked to treat a registered addict whom I had never seen before the day-by-day filming of the treatment began. He had a ten-year history of heroin addiction. If the NET treatment proved to be unsuccessful they still wished to show the film as publicized, but in that case they would analyze the causes of failure. The film team spent most of each day and evening in our home and my consulting room, filming various stages of the treatment and its effects on the patient. On the third day the patient gave the machine credit for aborting the withdrawal symptoms he had experienced at that stage when he had "cold-turkeyed" in the past, but added that he was "not feeling too good." On the fourth day, however, there was a dramatic change, and the film showed the patient relaxed and smiling, saying he was "feeling great."

Some patients required constant supervision in our own home, but I treated others as out-patients. When our landlord began to object to my treating patients at home over-night, I had to make arrangements for nearby nursing-homes or clinics to admit them. That was difficult, for very few wanted to take in drug addicts, and the special clinics for treating them were either already full or unwilling for various reasons to admit NET patients.

The official clinics for treating drug addictions, known as "the British system," were almost all out-patient facilities which provided registered addicts with daily supplies of methadone (Physeptone), a drug which had a cross-tolerance with morphine and heroin. (Only a few of these clinics still supply heroin.) The Methadone Maintenance Program of the British system was supposed to "enable addicts to adjust socially and occupationally without further criminal involvement," but only 5 percent of addicts on these programs refrained from simultaneous use of illegal drugs. Addicts disliked taking methadone regularly because they found it very much harder to discontinue methadone than heroin. This had been noted by expert researchers, one of whom stated categorically: "The tragedy of methadone is that we cannot get people off methadone."[12]

Alex Trocchi, author of *Cain's Book,* and himself a registered drug-dependent, saw clearly some of the problems of the official approach:

"If a doctor follows the recommendations of the Brain Report and tries to get his patient to accept a prescription for the smallest amount possible of the drug, an absurd situation arises. From the first interview the user feels forced to resort to cunning, to lying, to cheat, to beg, to fawn, in order to ensure adequate supplies. Doctor and patient are involved in a battle of wits in a destructive pseudo-problem, in which all the energies which should have been brought to bear upon the real problem are wastefully dissipated."[13]

Yet with NET I could get such patients off their methadone without distress, even from dosages as high as 800 milligrams daily. This was despite strongly negative expectations, for experienced methadone addicts did not believe it possible to stop all methadone for even a few days, let alone permanently.

All of this meant that I was having to treat patients in less-than-satisfactory circumstances, whether as out-patients or in-patients. But probably the most difficult and bizarre situation in all my experience began in 1977, four years after I had begun my research in London.

The Keith Richards case
The BBC had shown the first film on NET, called "Off the Hook" in 1975. In April 1977 they approached me about filming a follow-up of the patient treated in the first film which would answer the questions: how was he now? what was he doing? how far had NET progressed? I agreed to do it.

Just before this second film was completed I received an urgent telephone call from Canada asking me if I would treat Keith Richards of the rock music group "The Rolling Stones." There was nothing unusual about this, for I had already been approached about possible treatment for Keith, after treating Eric Clapton and others known to him. But this time, the circumstances in which I was being asked to treat him were unusual to the point of absurdity.

The newspapers had been full of an international scandal regarding Margaret Trudeau, wife of the Canadian Prime Minister, who allegedly spent a night or more at the hotel in Canada where the Rolling Stones were performing. New headlines replaced those when police discovered so much heroin in Keith Richards' hotel room that he was arrested, not merely for possession but for trafficking in drugs. That offense carried with it the possibility of twenty years in prison. There was considerable panic in the Rolling Stones' organization at the thought of their top musical performer being removed suddenly and committed to prison with the consequent break-up of the famous group and the potential loss of millions of dollars. It was an even greater shock to Keith, with his history of massive drug abuse and the expectation of having to go "cold-turkey" in prison.

The political complications associated with the Prime Minister's wife and her relationship with the Rolling Stones were superimposed on the political necessity for the authorities to be seen making a suitable example of the notorious rock star, Keith Richards. This made it more difficult than usual for me.

There were further complications. Because it was so politically sensitive, the conditions of Keith's bail required him to remain on the North American continent; and any attempt at treatment (with its implications of leniency) meant that the doctor involved in the treatment would have to be prepared to swear in court that he or she could cure addictions and give evidence in support of the claim. The Rolling Stones had not been able to find a physician in Canada or the United States who would accept Keith as a patient under such circumstances, so they telephoned me. Would I come to the United States and treat Keith there? I said I would.

I was able to find a clinic and two American colleagues willing to accept the difficult assignment, Dr. Richard Corbett and Dr. Joseph Winston. Dr. Corbett, with much experience in treating drug addictions, was Medical Director of the Lakeland Drug Abuse Clinic, in New Jersey. However, because of the political nature of the case the American authorities required us to describe our treatment plan for prior approval. We drew up a medical treatment protocol, for six weeks of detoxification and convalescence, which was acceptable to the U. S. Government. To avoid publicity, it was agreed that Keith should be treated privately in the nearby home of Shorty and Jean Yeaworth, film producer friends of ours.

Despite all the difficulties the treatment was successful, and the protocol signed by the three doctors—Corbett, Winston and myself—was accepted by the Canadian courts as evidence of the success of Keith's treatment, and he was not sent to prison.

No matter how simple NET might seem to a rock musician (see his comments on page 19), the NET stimulator was not "very simple." By then, electrical stimulation was being applied in a wide variety of treatment processes, sometimes in very complicated forms.

It had been established that the administration of electrical current in small amounts which were only mildly stimulating had beneficial effects in: epilepsy and spasticity (with electrodes implanted on the cerebellar cortex[14]); non-union of bone fractures (with electrodes implanted in the bone adjacent to the fracture site [15,16]); intractable skin ulcers (with electrodes applied to the ulcer[17]); anesthesia (with electrodes above the bridge of the nose and behind the ears[18]); control of chronic pain (with electrodes applied locally in the area of pain, or segmentally[19,20,21]); urinary incontinence (with electrodes inserted as a needle into the perineum or in an anal plug[22]); and to rehabilitate paralyzed muscles in multiple sclerosis (with percutaneous electrodes in the epidural space[23,24]).

When I began using electrical stimulation, I considered that the effect of stopping withdrawal symptoms could be explained by NET's action on the autonomic nervous system, mediated through the vagus nerve which has sensory connections with the external ear canal, the cranial surface of the auricle, and the skin in the region of the mastoid bone. However, this theory of direct parasympathetic modulation did not explain the relief of central signs and symptoms such as restlessness, irritability, muscle aches, yawning and insomnia.[25] Nor did it account for the later results of NET such as the abolition of craving for the drug of addiction after repeated short-term treatments, the increased optimism (in contrast to the usually depressed state of addicts treated by any other method), the freedom from dependence on any other therapeutically used drug, and the rapid and marked improvement in the patient's sleeping pattern without the use of any sedative drugs.

A good night's sleep

There seemed to be some association with Electro-Therapeutic Sleep, or Cerebral Electro-Therapy (CET), on which considerable research had been done in the Soviet Union and Europe in the past twenty years. The current in both NET and CET was passed through the brain, though in CET the electrodes were applied so that the current passed through the brain from the forehead region backwards,[26,27] instead of from side to side as in NET. CET had also been shown to be effective in cases of chronic anxiety, depression and insomnia.[28,29,30,31] Studies had been done with a control series,[32] or a double-blind control series, of patients suffering from neurotic anxiety and depression.[33]

An almost intractable problem in treating substance addictions is the insomnia that follows withholding of the drugs. Natural body rhythms have been so disturbed by drug and life-style abuse that normal patterns of sleep are non-existent. Addicts dread not only the restless nights but also the intense craving for drugs, and physical agony when they wake up after sleeping fitfully.

Drug addicts claim that it takes about two months to regain a normal sleep pattern after coming off heroin. This has been confirmed physiologically in volunteers who made themselves heroin-dependent.[34] Even though heroin was given to the volunteers for only seven consecutive nights, abnormalities of brain function were detectable for two months after withdrawal. The same study found that morphine suppressed REM sleep,[35] and there was a delayed REM sleep rebound on withdrawal. Some researchers claimed that it might take several months for various bodily functions to return to normal after withdrawal from opioids.[36,37]

Likewise, after withdrawal from amphetamines, sleep abnormalities take up to two months to disappear;[38] and after barbiturate withdrawal up to four months.[39] Daytime anxieties are reflected in nightmares during sleep. Research studies showed that after only a short period of using a small dose of nitrazepam for insomnia (Mogadon, 5 milligrams), the sleep pattern became more abnormal than it had been before the drug was begun, and reverted to its previous pattern only after one or two weeks.[40,41]

My NET patients were given electrical stimulation continuously day and night for the first five days. For that purpose, I developed new blunt electrodes, similar to those used in EKG applications, and fixed their adhesive surface on the mastoid bone behind the ears. When patients slept with these electrodes attached, NET effects came more rapidly, sleeping was restful and dreamless, and early morning discomfort was much reduced. Some patients said that NET did not put them to sleep, but that once they were asleep their sleep was deep and free from nightmares. I concluded that some synchronization was occurring between the brain's sleep rhythms and the therapeutic frequency. With these improved techniques, most addicts were able to achieve deep restful sleep by the third to the ninth night after commencing NET.[42]

More advanced stimulator models

My clinical experience with NET convinced me that the current frequency was the most important factor in treating addictions. Researchers in other applications of medical electronics were coming to similar conclusions.[43] (See Appendix XIV, p. 168.)

The importance of frequency was well-expressed by one well-known scientist: "The language of the brain is frequency. Some of the implications of this statement are beginning to be understood. Some observations we do not yet understand. When we learn to speak the frequency language of the brain, we may begin to understand what it is saying."[44]

By this time, the Shackman company, which had been so helpful, felt that my increasingly complex requirements were beyond their production capabilities and suggested that I try to find more expert help elsewhere. A friend introduced me to Peter Loose, whose company, European Electronic Systems, was doing advanced work in digital technology. Although the company had no experience in what I was doing, Peter was interested and willing to help.

I explained the increasingly complex electronic mechanism I now required to effect the desired responses in the patients; this involved combinations and permutations which I had never imagined in my early days of research. So began almost two years' research and experimentation to produce a smaller but more sophisticated and accurate machine than the "Shackman-Patterson" models. I called them the "Pharmakon-Patterson NeuroElectric Stimulator," Models III and IV.

The development of those machines began soon after I had treated Keith Richards and continued until we opened the Pharmakon Clinic in January 1980, for clinical trials.

The second BBC film, "Still Off The Hook," had been televised in July 1977. It included an interview with the American doctor, Richard Corbett, eulogizing NET and mentioning that I was being invited to the United States. The broadcast of that film had a dramatic effect. It produced an outcry against my leaving Britain and taking NET to the United States; and it attracted the interest of The Rank Foundation, which offered to fund my research and clinical trials in Britain. It also brought support from other foundations.

It took almost two years to set up a Clinic, train an appropriate staff, and prepare the paperwork for future analyses in a treatment process which was so totally new. I devoted myself to preparing the medical instruction and analytical material, while my husband, George, prepared the material for the psycho-spiritual rehabilitation which would compliment the rapid detoxification by NET.

During this period, I also met with the late Director of the Marie Curie Memorial Foundation, Dr. Don Williams, to discuss possibilities for doing research work on animal models at their Sussex laboratories, investigating the effects of NET in cancer-linked conditions, such as stress, and cigarette and alcohol abuse.

As I made progress in solving detoxification problems, I became increasingly conscious of the psycho-spiritual problems associated with addiction. I knew that the endorphins were closely linked with the emotions. That meant that as we restored the body's chemistry by electrical stimulation we also had to deal with its renewed capacity to respond to psychological and physiological stimuli, and to stress.

The few existing drug rehabilitation centers and therapeutic communities were booked solidly in advance for several months. Few churches seemed to be concerned, and those that were concerned were not equipped to provide the informed and structured counseling necessary for drug addicts and alcoholics. There were voluntary organizations for marriage guidance, for potential suicides, and for family counseling, but none of them had personnel trained to cope with drug addicts and alcoholics in a specialized "recovery program."

We felt strongly that to deal only with detoxification of the addict was irresponsible; and to deal only with the psycho-spiritual problem of the addict was naive. Both aspects of the problem had to be addressed, and a system including both detoxification and rehabilitation had to be devised. I was already being challenged by the proliferating processes, ranging from the mechanical to the spiritual, such as biofeedback, placebos, and various belief systems which were surfacing during my investigations of endorphins, and their relation to addictions. Some of these new frontiers might have a possible part to play in the effective treatment of addictions.

PART II
REDEFINING
ADDICTIONS

7 What
Is Addiction?

Nobody really knows what causes addiction—least of all the psychiatrists, the professionals who are supposed to know the most about it—but, as with the common cold, almost everybody is the victim of addiction in some form at some time. Nobody minds admitting to having experienced the common cold, yet very few are prepared to admit to being addicts. Yet addiction is now recognized officially as the world's greatest social problem.

Addiction—a diverse phenomenon
The official Report of the Council of Europe (Strasbourg, 1970) (see p. 155), represented by nineteen countries studying the drug problems of Europe, concluded: "...in all countries there has been an upsurge in the number of drug dependents which has now attained the dimensions of an epidemic," and went on to state:

"It is important to have in mind that this subject includes not only psychological and medical but also social, educational, cultural, and political aspects. The increase in the dimensions of the problems can be looked upon as a symptom indicating that there is something very wrong with society. The problem 'is a problem neither of youth nor one of drugs, but a problem of a whole society and an entire life-style shared by young and old alike' " (quoting the evidence of a doctor before a U.S. Senate Committee on the Judiciary, September 17, 1969).

Beside addictions caused by the use of illegal drugs such as heroin, cocaine and hashish, and the abuse of prescription drugs such as tranquilizers, amphetamines and barbiturates, other addictive substances and habits abound. In Britain admissions to hospitals of alcohol-related problems increased twenty-fold in the past twenty years. In the United States alcohol-related problems cost $25 billion a year. In the Soviet Union almost sixty percent of the work force has some form of alcoholism. In Zambia about a third of all fatalities were caused by alcoholism. In Venezuela about two-thirds of road casualties were caused by alcohol.

In the United States nicotine-related diseases cost $5 to $8 billion a year, not to mention another $15 million due to lost wages and productivity. It was reckoned in Britain that there were over seventeen million nicotine addicts — that is, people who had tried more than three times to give up smoking and had failed.

It cost Britain's National Health Service some $20 million to pay for the fifty million prescriptions by doctors annually of anti-anxiety tranquilizers.

Then there are the uncountable millions of tea and coffee addicts, those who need eight or more cups a day for "more rapid and clearer flow of thought, to allay drowsiness, to increase motor activity, or to produce a keener appreciation of sensory stimuli," as one medical definition described it. When withdrawn, tea and coffee were also found to produce the symptoms of addiction: "fits of agitation, depression, loss of color, haggard appearance, loss of appetite, heart palpitation and irregularity." In a U.S. government laboratory experiment with caffeine, the basic ingredient of tea and coffee, the offspring of rats which were fed the equivalent of twelve to twenty-four cups of coffee daily had an unusually high proportion of missing or deformed toes; there was even some delay in skeletal development in the offspring of rats fed the equivalent of two cups of coffee daily.

Nor does this exhaust the list of the addicted. There are work-alcoholics who dare not stop working because of the psychological and physiological consequences; there are the gamblers who bet on horses, cards, bingo, slot machines; there are compulsive eaters, television viewers (one study showed the usual withdrawal symptoms during thirty days of TV "abstinence"); there are video-game players and all varieties of cult adherents.

All of these are just different aspects and emphases of a destructive mon-omania in an anxiety-ridden twentieth century seeking cures for its empti-ness and meaninglessness.

In Britain the popular newspapers troubled with dropping circulations introduced "newspaper bingo," and the results were "phenomenal," ac-cording to a report in the London *Observer*, "putting on sales at the rate of 100,000 a month." It continued: "Bingo is not only a national habit, it has addictive properties, and once people are involved in a game they tend to persist to the end."

Addiction, therefore, is a complex problem with roots in the individual, family, and society, sometimes coming to the surface early in life and some-times much later. There is not sufficient evidence to indicate anything so strong as the "addictive personality" postulated by some psychiatrists. However, one common feature has been found among drug addicts ob-served in the addiction epidemics in Japan as well as in North America—an absent, weak, or inadequate father.

The anatomy of addiction

An addict is someone who cannot deal with people or circumstances in his or her immediate environment, because of personal inadequacy. Philo-sophically, it has been suggested that: *adaequatio rei et intellectus* — "the understanding of the knower must be adequate to the thing to be known." In everyday terms we are talking about the inability of the individual to cope with family, school, office, workshop, boardroom, household, or so-cial occasion without the "support" of some chemical substance.

Without the cigarette, drink, or drug such an individual soon becomes a very anti-social creature, cogently described by one noted authority:

"Addicted patients are asocial, inadequate, immature and unstable. They are selfish and self-centered without interest in the welfare of others and are only concerned with their own problems. Their major problem is in their maintenance of the supply of drugs or the immediate gratification of their desire for drugs. They will resort to any means — however unrea-sonable or dangerous — to satisfy this insistent craving. They have failed to develop normal human relationships and are almost totally without con-cern for the distress they inflict on their relatives. They lack self-discipline, will-power or ambition, and avoid responsibility. They have a low thresh-old for pain or any form of discomfort, and are unable to tolerate criticism or to bear frustration. Their personal relationships tend to become confined to other members of the drug addicts' world, and thus they become social outcasts and very lonely people."[1]

Incisive as this analysis is, it is still only a superficial description of an addict; it does not penetrate deep enough to provide a true explanation of the problem from which to move towards a possible solution. It is necessary to explore the intricacies of social structures, family relationships and, ultimately, the mind of individual addicts. The whole person must be understood — body, mind, and *spirit* (a dimension rarely acknowledged by psychiatrists although, significantly, emphasized with a greater measure of success by the more spiritually-oriented Alcoholics Anonymous) — in order to reach some understanding of the cause and so begin to develop a cure.

Even in laboratory experiments with rats some of the complexities of addictions were observed. Laboratory animals would starve themselves of food rather than cross an electrified grid to reach it; but they would cross that same electrified grid in order to reach a pleasure-stimulus. Other rats were tested with pans of plain water or of heroin solution; the "leader" rat, and "lower-rank" rats, after tasting both, kept to the pans of plain water, but the "middle-rank" rats chose the heroin solution. In yet another experiment, rats which were deprived of all forms of stress gradually lost interest in food, then in sex, and eventually became impotent and died.

Of course, it does not follow *ipso facto* that what is true of rats is also true of humans, but the experimental evidence is at least suggestive: that stress and challenge are necessary elements in life, but that to some more than others, intense stresses cause them to choose the relief of a narcotic, and that, given a choice between food or pleasure, some will opt for pleasure at the risk of possible death. These circumstances were imposed on the rats for the purposes of experiments; humans choose of their own accord to follow similar patterns.

Still other generalizations can be made from observations recorded by those who work with addicts. 70 percent of addicts have no strong and caring father. Either or both parents of an addict are two to seven times more likely than the parents of a non-addict to have been on some kind of mood-altering drugs, such as tranquilizers. Most addicts have parents who were either above-average alcohol drinkers, or heavy smokers, or both; most addicts have had anxiety-provoking home circumstances or a history of resorting to legal medications in the past.

Dr. David Smith, who founded the Haight-Ashbury Free Medical Clinic in San Francisco in 1967, has stated that the child of an alcoholic parent is thirty-five times more likely than the child of a non-alcoholic to become addicted himself, and that this ratio soars to 400 if both parents were alcoholics.[2]

To sum it up in a single sentence: the addict is someone whose personal belief or experience is inadequate to his or her chosen environment; but who, in resorting to chemicals, objects, persons, or ritualized activities for escape or relief, becomes addicted to the experience created by these substitutes.

Dr. Stanton Peele, in his book *Love and Addiction,* has described it this way:

"An addict is a person who never learns to come to grips with his world, and who therefore seeks stability and reassurance through some repeated, ritualized activity. This activity is reinforced in two ways: first, by a comforting sensation of well-being induced by the drug or other addictive object; second, by the atrophy of the addict's other interests and abilities and the general deterioration of his life situation while he is preoccupied with his addiction. As alternatives grow smaller the addiction grows larger, until it is all there is. A true addict progresses into monomania, whether the object of addiction is a drug or a lover..."[3]

Addiction, therefore, is *alienation* — from parents, or children, or friends, or churches, or God. Addiction is *emptiness* — a vast and tedious apathy, a meaningless continuum, a sense of insignificance, or anonymity, or purposelessness. Addiction is *inadequacy* — in personal relationships, or studies, or employment, or housework; it is inability to perform the smallest responsible task. Addiction is *guilt* — about failure as parent, or child, or husband, or wife, or manager, or employee; as cynic or sycophant, as leader or led, as teacher or student, as artist or artisan, as neighbor or colleague.

Dr. Peele expands his definition of an addict:

"...In these terms, then, an addiction exists when a person's attachment to a sensation, an object, or another person is such as to lessen his appreciation of and ability to deal with other things in his environment, or in himself, so that he has become increasingly dependent on that experience as his only source of gratification. A person will be predisposed to addiction to the extent that he cannot establish a meaningful relationship to his environment as a whole, and thus cannot develop a fully elaborated life."[3]

Dependence is not addiction

A common mistake among those involved with addicts is to confuse "dependence" with "addiction." It is possible to be dependent on a drug and not to be addicted. For example, the diabetic who is dependent on insulin injections and uses a syringe regularly, does not become "addicted" to the drug with its classic symptoms; nor does the regularity of his insulin injections become the ritualized obsession of the heroin addict.

The distinction is important and involves the dimension of bondage or freedom. Dependence is the relationship between an individual and a drug that is ultimately beneficial (many diabetics on insulin become international athletes); while addiction is the relationship between an individual, a drug, and society, that is ultimately destructive (that is, it involves a violation of social norms in patterns of lying, deceit and often stealing). Dependence can be and usually is a healthy experience, as is, for example, the loving inter-dependence between husband and wife, or between children and parents, or between members of a community or church; but when any of these relationships become self-centered and exploitative a new element is introduced, and the relationship becomes one of destructive bondage instead of productive freedom.

Addiction = bondage

Whatever else it is, therefore, addiction is *bondage*. (Actually, that is what the word meant before psychiatrists confused the condition with pseudo-scientific jargon.) The word "addiction" in English language and literature means "bondage." In his book, *Licit and Illicit Drugs*, Edward M. Brecher states this very clearly:

"In Roman law to be addicted meant to be bound over to someone by a judicial sentence; thus the prisoner of war might be addicted to some nobleman or large landowner. In sixteenth century England, the word had the same meaning; thus a serf might be addicted to a master. But Shakespeare and others of his era perceived the marked similarity between this legal form of addiction and a man's bondage to alcoholic beverages; they therefore spoke of being 'addicted to alcohol.' Poets also spoke of men 'addicted to vice,' and of women 'addicted to virginity.' Dr. Johnson spoke of 'addiction to tobacco,' and John Stuart Mill of 'addiction to bad habits.' The conception of addiction to opium, morphine, and heroin followed quite naturally."[4]

It was mainly because of their inability to understand this important dimension, or unwillingness to address the problem from this standpoint, that many doctors and psychiatrists involved with the treatment of addictions fell into the trap of mechanical mind-tinkering and pill-pushing, with its present disastrous consequences.

One of the world's most famous addicts is the well-known playwright, Jean Cocteau, who wrote a revealing book out of his own experiences. *Opium: The Diary of an Addict* describes his harrowing attempts to come off the drug, and the doctors' attempts to cure him:

"Incredible phenomena are attached to the cure; medicine is powerless against them, beyond making the padded cell look like a hotel-room and demanding of the doctor or nurse patience, attendance and sensitivity...

"I therefore became an opium addict again because of the doctors who cure — one should really say, quite simply, who purge — do not seek to cure the troubles which first cause the addiction...

"After the cure. The worst moment, the worst danger. Health with this void and an immense sadness. The doctors honestly hand you over to suicide.

"Now that I am cured, I feel empty, poor, heart-broken and ill..."[5]

What a literate, devastating indictment! Other addicts less articulate than Jean Cocteau, but just as aware of the many forms of treatment practiced on them, and the varied medications prescribed by doctors, could echo his words: "Now that I am 'cured,' I feel empty, poor, heart-broken and ill." From laudanum to Librium, from morphine to methadone, from alcohol to Ativan, the "cures" for addiction simply evade the two main questions implicit in the problem of addiction: How may an addict be detoxified from bondage to chemicals? and, How may the underlying emptiness of life be filled?

If addiction is to be truly cured the emptiness must be filled, meaning must be provided, capacity to love and forgive must be developed, repentance must be encouraged, ability to think must be taught, willingness to take responsibility must be cultivated, hope must be implanted, the seeds of faith and vision must be sown. Ultimately, God must be recognized as real; the individual cannot be left at the mercy of an amorphous, uncaring "force." Beyond a bottle, a pill, a powder, an injection, an object, a cause, a ritual, a sensation, all addicts are looking for God. What they really want is love, or truth, or beauty, or joy, or life, or transcendence, or power — or God.

The emptiness of the addict

In the 1930s the eminent psychoanalyst Dr. Carl Jung commented: "About a third of my cases are suffering from no clinically definable neurosis, but from the senselessness and emptiness of their lives. It seems that this can be described as the greatest neurosis of our time."[6]

This emptiness has not diminished. If anything, it has increased, so that Dr. Rollo May could write some years ago:

"It may seem surprising when I say, on the basis of my own clinical practice, as well as that of my psychological and psychiatric colleagues, that the chief problem of the middle decade of the twentieth century is emptiness...While one might laugh at the meaningless boredom of people a decade or so ago, the emptiness for many has now moved from the state of boredom to a state of futility and despair which holds promise of dangers..."[7]

This is the "sickness" of Western society which was apparent to the members who wrote up the Report of the Council of Europe on drug addiction, and which is the true root of the problem: emptiness and meaninglessness. This can be demonstrated by joining Dr. Peele's definition of addiction with Paul Tillich's definition of "the emptiness of society."

"The anxiety of emptiness is aroused by the threat of non-being to the special contents of the spiritual life. A belief breaks down through external events or inner processes: one is cut off from creative participation in a sphere of culture, one feels frustrated about something which one has passionately affirmed, one is driven from devotion to one object to devotion to another and again on to another, because the meaning of each of them vanishes and the creative eros is transformed into indifference or aversion. Everything is tried and nothing satisfies... Anxiously one turns away from all concrete contents and looks for an ultimate meaning, only to discover that it was the loss of a spiritual center which took away the meaning from the special contents of the spiritual life...The anxiety of emptiness drives us to the abyss of meaninglessness."[8]

Thus, when addicts have been detoxified — or, rather, "dried out," or "cold-turkeyed," but not really detoxified in the true sense of the term — from their particular chemical of addiction, or de-programmed from their particular ritualized addictive activity, it is glaringly apparent that they are not *cured*, as Jean Cocteau so graphically stated. They are only removed temporarily from the *consequences* of a particular form of addictive indulgence or behavior. Unfortunately, it is just at this point of being relieved of a particular consequence that the addict is usually discharged by the doctor or therapist as "cured" — when both know that the actual cause of addiction has not even been touched.

Needed — a new framework

The real cure of such an individual requires a restructured life, a therapeutic rehabilitation which will provide an adequate framework of values to give meaning to the individual and help towards an understanding of his or her place in society. This framework includes a freedom to choose, a confidence to make the choice, and a responsibility to pay the price of that choice. It requires that the individual be provided with a framework of knowledge "adequate to the thing to be known," in order that the underlying emptiness and meaninglessness in their lives, due to the previous lack of adequate values, be cured. To do this successfully requires a form of psychotherapy hitherto not known; or, if known, certainly not widely practiced. We will enlarge on this in a later chapter.

As has already been noted, emptiness and meaninglessness are spiritual problems, and psychiatry—certainly Freudian psychoanalysis and behaviorism—considers any concern with the spiritual a form of neurosis in itself. This negativism implicit in current psychotherapeutic processes often adversely contributes to the addictive mindset because of inherent philosophical inadequacies.

Time Magazine, in its April 25, 1983 issue, describes how Dr. George Vaillant, a Harvard psychiatrist, evaluates traditional psychiatric approaches to the problem of alcoholism: "They are nearly useless in dealing with the underlying nature of alcoholism itself. In his book *[The Natural History of Alcoholism: Causes, Patterns, and Paths to Recovery],* Vaillant ruefully describes his own disillusionment with his profession's ability to cope with the disease. 'I was working for the most exciting alcohol program in the world,' he says, "But the results at the clinic were no better than if the doctors had left the alcoholics alone."

"Other professionals agree with Vaillant's glum assessment. 'We don't do anything adequately,' admits Dr. Robert Millman, director of the Alcohol and Drug Abuse Service at Payne Whitney Psychiatric Clinic in New York City.

"What about expensive hospital treatment centers, now so fashionable that they have become a growth industry with companies listed on the New York Stock Exchange? Vaillant concludes flatly that they do not work in the long run."

The *Time* article concludes: ". . . even though it's terribly unscientific, alcoholics usually do seem to need some kind of source of hope and self-esteem, or religious inspiration—whatever you want to call it—and that seems more important than hospital or psychiatric care."[9]

In his book, *Drugs: Medical, Psychological and Social Facts*, Peter Lawrie declares:

"Addicts are notoriously resistant to ordinary psychotherapy. One way of looking at this is to observe that analysis depends on communication, on the patient's acceptance of the therapist as a real human being who can have a real effect on him. But the addict's whole life is organized to remove any dependence on humanity: given his drugs, he is self-sufficient, able to generate his own satisfactions and guilts and to live a rich emotional life independent of the outside world. He therefore has no motives for communication when things are going well; when he does present himself for treatment it is often not because he wants to be cured of addiction, but because his addiction is not working as it should. He is a two-time loser who wants to get back to being a one-time loser, not to take the much more perilous step to being an unloser. The ordinary psychiatric patient is like a burr, offering many hooks to the world and the therapist—often too many; the therapist's best strategy is to stand still and let his patient attach himself as he will. But the addict is like a nut: smooth, with a thick armor. The only hook he offers is his need for drugs, and that can be satisfied in a number of ways. To reach the addict, his shell must be cracked. We might guess that it would be necessary to counter the coercion of opiates with the coercion of therapy..."[1]

It was absolutely necessary, therefore, that a satisfactory form of chemical detoxification take place before any serious attempt at psychotherapy was attempted. What passed for "detoxification" of addictions was a debasement of the term; addicts might be "dried out," or "cold-turkeyed," in a variety of institutions devoted to what was publicized as detoxification, but they were certainly not detoxified in the true sense of the term (which, etymologically speaking, means removing a poisoned arrow).

Dr. Avram Goldstein, an international authority on addictions, had made this clear:

"It is still not understood why simple detoxification is so ineffective, but the facts are clear and inescapable...As I see it, the reason for the dismal failure of detoxification (the majority of subjects relapse before completing the customary 21- to 30-day process) is that the newly detoxified addict, still driven by discomfort, physiologic imbalances, and intense craving, cannot focus attention on the necessary first steps towards rehabilitation, but soon succumbs and starts using heroin again..."[10]

Complete detoxification of the addict, therefore, was important at this stage. Freed from the exhaustingly assertive physiological imbalances and intense craving the mind could then turn without distraction to the deeper problems underlying the chemical or behavioral addictions.

It was clear that the detoxification process itself would have to come from outside the pharmaceutical industry, with its vested interests in chemotherapy which simply replaced the initial chemically addictive condition with a different and often more dangerous chemically addictive substance.

The discovery we had made in Hong Kong, that an electrical stimulus was somehow capable of curing opium and heroin addicts of the detoxification aspects of their addiction, opened up new possibilities. We were being presented with an opportunity to break the captive cycle which had kept so many in bondage for so long, and to cross a new frontier. Scientists from the East and West were discovering the importance of electrical impulses in the brain and body mechanisms.

Somehow it was appropriate that it was in Hong Kong, and from China, that this first clue arose, for it was from Hong Kong in the nineteenth century that the British authorities and traders had carried the opium that was to corrupt and destroy the lives of many millions in China. In the twentieth century the possible cure for that addiction had been brought from China to Hong Kong. Now I was carrying it back to Britain.

8 THE PLACEBO EFFECT AND BELIEF SYSTEMS

While it is known what a placebo is, how a placebo works is not fully understood. A placebo is an inert substance used to test new drugs in medical trials. However, it is coming to be realized that placebos not only can be made to appear like medicines but can also act like medicine in a way that baffles scientists. Placebos have even been known to "cure" malignant conditions and it is for this reason that doctors and scientists are highly suspicious of medicines like Laetrile, which has been claimed, without proof, to be a cancer cure.

The "placebo effect" was the reason most often given by some psychiatrists and doctors to explain away my apparent successes. None of them, incidentally, had ever been in touch with me; or, from the impression gathered from their comments in the media when they were interviewed regarding my work, had they even read about it.

Another consensus of medical opinion about my work with NET, gathered by a well-known charity in Britain which was considering funding my research, even went so far as to maintain that my successes could be explained by the fact that I was "a healer." I can well imagine the kind of response I would have had from the same group of doctors had I made personal claims to being "a healer"!

The witty and penetrating writer Adam Smith, in his book, *Powers of Mind,* said: "Placebo is *I shall be pleasing* in Latin, and nothing at all in pharmacology. It is a fake. Sugar and water. It's there to fool the mind. Of course, you have to believe the placebo is real, and clever psychologists have even tested what is most real in their nothing pill... The clever psychologists compared placebos and pain relievers in a double blind, where neither the experimenter nor pill taster knew what was what, and the placebo were 50-something percent as effective as practically everything! 54 percent as aspirin, 54 percent as Darvon (a tranquilizer), 56 percent as morphine. Two placebos work better than one. Placebo injections work better than placebo pills. Placebos work better when they aren't given by doctors because doctors like to give real medicine and not sugar pills, and the patient gets the unverbalized message from the doctor's face and tone: the vibes give it away."[1]

The word "placebo" has been used since 1811 to describe an inert, innocuous medication, or "a medicine given more to please than to benefit the patient." In other words, a "dummy tablet." The term is also used of a doctor with "an effective bedside manner," a warm personality, an enthusiastic conviction.

Norman Cousins's experience

The placebo effect was also claimed by reactionary doctors to explain the remarkable recovery of Norman Cousins, the distinguished editor of *Saturday Review.* Flying home to the United Stated from a physically and mentally demanding visit to Moscow he became ill with a mysterious condition which baffled all the doctors he consulted. After exhaustive tests and two weeks in hospital he was at the point of death. A report left by one doctor for another and read by Cousins said: "I'm afraid we may be losing Norman." None of the consultants could give a precise diagnosis, although there was a consensus among them that he was suffering from a serious collagen illness — a disintegration of the connective tissue between the cells. For this they gave him two dozen aspirins a day, sleeping pills to sleep, and pain-relieving drugs. His own doctor told him he had only one chance in 500 of recovering from this mysterious condition.

It was at that point that Cousins took matters into his own hands. He sent for books on stress, and read; "If negative emotions produce negative chemical changes, then positive emotions could produce positive changes." Discharging himself from hospital and booking a hotel room, he sent for some Marx Brothers' movies and a film projector and took himself off all drugs. He says that every night he literally laughed himself to sleep. He sent for and took massive doses of vitamin C intravenously. He read many humorous books such as *The Enjoyment of Laughter.*

Writing his own account of the experience Cousins said: "Two or three doctors have commented that I was probably the beneficiary of a mammoth venture in self-administered placebos. Such a hypothesis bothers me not at all. Respectable names in the history of medicine, like Paracelsus and Osler, have suggested that the history of medication is far more the history of the placebo effect than of intrinsically valuable and relevant drugs. . ."[2]

Unnecessary drugs

The evidence shows that nature itself is the best healing process, with the doctor as the best healing agent — that is, the doctor as he or she was before aspirin was discovered in 1899 and rarely as he or she is today. In 1962, when the United States Food and Drug Administration examined the 4,300 prescription drugs that had appeared since World War II, only two out of five were found to be effective. A few years ago in Britain an official circular sent to all medical practitioners stated that after six weeks' continuous use, Valium ceased to be effective and became addictive; yet tens of thousands of doctors continue to prescribe Valium regularly for their unwitting patients—many of whom are probably warning their teenage offspring about the dangers of becoming addicted to marijuana. To patients who regularly take Valium I say: "Try coming off the drug for a few days and watch what happens; you will have all the symptoms of withdrawal."

It has been estimated by experienced clinicians that between twenty to fifty drugs are all that will ever be needed for 98 percent of the population. Dr. Vernon Coleman, in his book, *The Medicine Men,* reports seven out of ten British doctors prescribe placebos for unhappiness, and quotes a statement that family doctors in Britain estimate that up to a third of their patients have nothing wrong with them and are simply unhappy.[3]

Dr. Colin Brewer, writing in *World Medicine,* noted that, with the exception of schizophrenics, patients taking part in clinical trials of psychiatric drugs often respond in greater numbers to the placebo than specifically to the active drug. He commented that, in the relatively mild disorders which account for most psychiatric problems seen in general practice, it was common to find that 40 to 50 percent of the patients responded to the placebo, and it was rare for the proportion who responded to the active drug to exceed this figure by more than 10 or 20 percent. He added:

"We know, furthermore, that it is not even necessary to administer drugs to make patients feel better. A trial of dynamic psychotherapy versus behaviour therapy revealed that the control group, who merely had a thorough psychiatric history taken and were then placed on a waiting list, improved to the tune of 70 percent; in many respects this was as good as the psychodynamic patients, and almost as good as the behavioural group."[4]

In a letter to the *British Medical Journal* Dr. J. Guy Edwards declared:

"In 15 studies involving 1082 patients with a wide variety of organic and psychiatric disorders placebos had an average significant effectiveness of 35.2 percent and were most effective when stress was greatest. In the Medical Research Council's trial of the treatment of depressive illness about a third of the patients receiving placebo 'wholly or almost wholly lost their symptoms' within the first four weeks."[5]

This leaves many patients who would recover without the administration of drugs, but because of the withdrawal they experience when trying to stop these drugs, they think that the drugs are still necessary.

There is little doubt in my own mind that the placebo effect plays a significant role in substance abuse as it does even in cancer, from whatever stimulus. In some ways still unknown to us, the brain is able to pick up a message which it then transforms by conviction into biochemical changes. And since there are stress factors involved in cancer and in substance abuse, the appropriate stimulus to effect amelioration of these stress factors is of critical importance. The "appropriate stimulus," in medical terms, could be either electromagnetic or chemical; but in philosophical terms it is associated with information and the strength and quality of belief in the information, however it is communicated.

Does NET depend on the placebo effect?
However, few patients who have requested NET believed that an electrical stimulus could deal with an obsession as powerful as heroin—or cigarettes. They had lost the ability to believe, and their will-power had been dissipated by years of self-indulgence. Placebo alone was insufficient to bridge the gap between belief and will-power.

In animal experiments, the placebo factor is eliminated. Rats and mice addicted to morphine suffer withdrawal symptoms similar to those of humans: electrostimulation through the rats' ears significantly relieved the symptoms of withdrawal in these animals.[6,7]

Thus it is clear to me that the successes of NET cannot be attributed only, or mainly, to the placebo effect.

In the past few years, in the field of alcoholism, interesting experiments have been carried out at a number of American universities in what one report called "the Think Drink Effect." For example, if a person thinks he is drinking alcohol but is really drinking only tonic he will exhibit the same sort of uninhibited behavior that he would normally attribute to the effects of alcohol.[8]

The psychological rationale behind these experiments was that a drinker is expecting a high; because of past experience, when he drinks he has a combination of physical effects of the alcohol and psychological expectations about it. This is compared to the well-known Pavlovian reaction—a dog salivates at the sound of a bell associated with the smell and taste of food; so the experienced drinker may achieve a conditioned high when presented with the cue properties of a drink (appearance, smell, and taste) even when the simulated drink contains no alcohol whatever.

One study of inexperienced drinkers, involving 1500 students aged twelve to nineteen, showed that actual experience was not necessary to have expectations of a high, ranging from reduction of tension to social pleasure to alteration of behavior.

In another study, thirty-two volunteers were divided into four groups: members of one group were told they were drinking alcohol but were actually drinking a non-alcoholic beverage similar in taste and appearance; one group was told they were not drinking alcohol and they were not; one group was told they were not drinking alcohol but they were; one group was told they were drinking alcohol and they were. From the study it was concluded that people's beliefs about alcohol were just as important as other factors. However, alcohol expectation affected only social behaviors such as conversation, sexual arousal and aggressiveness, and did not affect such skills as driving.

In a report in *The Lancet*, a research group in California investigated the possibility that placebos might act by stimulating the release of endorphins, in which case the effect should be abolished by an antagonist such as naloxone which blocks opioid receptors. This hypothesis was tested with a number of dental patients, some on morphine and some on a placebo. About 40 percent of the patients given a placebo reported relief of their pain. However, when they were given naloxone as a second injection these patients said that the pain became worse. In contrast, naloxone made little or no difference to the patients who had not responded to the placebo. Also, when naloxone was given as the first injection it not only failed to relieve pain but also reduced the likelihood of a placebo response to later injections.[9] The Science column of the London *Times* of Sept. 23, 1978, reported on this:

"This evidence provides strong support for the theory that placebo effects are mediated through endorphins. If indeed that is the mechanism it would explain some of the similarities between placebos and narcotic drugs. Both become less effective with repeated use; there is a tendency for the dose needed to rise with time; and withdrawal symptoms may develop when the opiate or placebo is stopped."

It is now believed that endorphins play an important role in regulating our awareness of and response to pain, mood, and *level of motivation for various kinds of purposeful behavior.* After patients have been detoxified by NET, it is essential that an adequate psycho-spiritual support system be provided. Meditation on spiritual values is the most effective way in which this can be inculcated.

Meditation
One of the pioneer investigators of endorphins was the late Dr. Nathan Kline of the Rockfield Research Institute, New York, who noted the relationship of meditation to biochemical changes:

"It is absolutely zero surprise that hormones change in meditation. The idea of mind and body as two separate entities. . .is artificial. It would be highly surprising if mind and body didn't have a relation to each other. The basic unit is the organism, not the mind somehow joined to the body."

There are now many reputable medical and scientific groups in different parts of the world studying the effects of Transcendental Meditation and its possible uses in everyday medical practice. One listed report of a three-year study was given by Dr. Bernard C. Glueck who presented an evaluation of the phenomena observed during the process of meditation. He said that there were a number of striking findings that seemed to be unique to this particular technique in the sense that the changes appeared more consistently, with greater rapidity, and to a much greater degree—referring primarily to the EEG changes observed in TM meditators, compared to those of individuals using other types of meditation, and non-meditating resting subjects.

In an article entitled "Relief of Psychiatric Symptoms in Evangelical Religious Sects," which dealt with the emergence of numerous religious sects in the United States and Western Europe in the past decade, the authors concluded:

"Analysis of questionnaires revealed that members of the sects had experienced psychological difficulties prior to conversion. Many had sought professional help for these...and some even hospitalization...Members also reported a high incidence of drug use before joining. Approximately one quarter of the respondents in the groups answered in the affirmative to having had serious drug problems in the past...The proportion who had used drugs of abuse to any extent was much higher than that for a comparable national sample. For example, when compared with a matched group in a national survey about twice as many Divine Light Mission members had ever taken each of the groups of drugs, for example 92 versus 52 percent for marijuana and 14 versus 6 percent for heroin...

"However, with conversion a marked change in these parameters was reported. Such change was reflected in neurotic symptom scores noted for the period before joining as compared with those after joining...*It does indeed appear that the conversion of one's system of beliefs leads to a certain relief of psychological distress*...The study of charismatic sects teaches us the importance of maintaining a mutually accepted system of norms and beliefs for treatment personnel as well as for patients. *If we attempt to effect change without addressing a patient's value systems we risk coming up against impenetrable difficulties...*" [10] (my italics)

But it is important to note that whatever spiritual belief system an individual chooses it must be adequate to meet, and overcome if necessary, the challenges of the environment in which the individual lives and functions. Otherwise it serves only as a talismanic superstition, and not as an effective value system for change.

Superficial religious formulae
Professional religionists with easy formulae have seriously damaged their cause as well as their own reputations with their talismanic versions of Christianity. The difficult process of acquiring spiritual enlightenment has

been movingly described by the Russian Marxist-turned-Christian philosopher, Nikolai Berdyaev:

"The suffering that has once been lived through cannot possibly be effaced... The man who has travelled far in the realms of the spirit, and who has passed through great trials in the cause of his search for truth, will be formed spiritually along lines which must differ altogether from those pertaining to the man who has never shifted his position and to whom new spiritual territories are unknown...I am enriched by my experience, even if it has been fearful and tormenting, even if to cross the abyss I have been forced to address myself to powers other than human..."[11]

Meaningful relationships

Our own family experience of this in various countries, as we sought to understand and obey the will of God, had given us a unique experience of how to deal with people afflicted with "emptiness and meaninglessness" in their lives, whether they were drug addicts or not. But with each addicted patient I treated there was no doubt that the root problem was psycho-spiritual, characterized by some form of emptiness and meaninglessness, and that they despaired of finding ultimate answers. What was there to live for? Why should they come off drugs? How would they cope at home, at work, at play, without them? Who would want to live in such a lousy world without drugs? What was the point of talking about a relationship with a father, a mother, a wife, a husband, a lover, children, friends or God? Who cared whether you lived or died anyway? In their minds the emptiness stretched and deepened into an unbridgeable gulf.

But as we spoke of the spiritual values of love, forgiveness, repentance, mercy, joy, peace, and salvation for all, what began as cynicism from even the most hardened individual moved slowly to wary consideration, and often advanced to tentative or glad acceptance. Living in close contact with others in the Pharmakon community, they could see people whose lives did have meaning, who did care. It was not just empty moralizing.

Whenever a patient would come right up front and say, for example, "The thing is, I just hate my father and can't come to terms with him," we would try to deal with that individual's problem. We would contact the father, bring parent and child together, and try to point out that forgiveness is an essential part of the healing mechanism. It wasn't enough for parents to want a son or daughter to come off a drug. They had to deal with whatever element, actions, or attitudes were exacerbating the problem. We could spell out the steps we perceived as necessary for recovery, but the recovery first required forgiveness on their part. The statement of Jesus that a person must first forgive in order to receive God's forgiveness—and a new life—is no mere platitude (Matthew 6:14-15).

So, when other patients saw that one patient had forgiven his domineering father, another a promiscuous mother, or another an overindulgent mother, after years of hating those parents: or when they saw an addict come off heavy doses of heroin and cocaine because of his real love for a woman; or when a son came off heroin because the father he had never known found him after eighteen years' search—those patients saw the spiritual values in action, not merely in words.

Logotherapy and "the will-to-meaning"
Dr. Viktor E. Frankl has pioneered logotherapy, which some writers have called "the third Viennese School of Psychotherapy." (See Appendix XV, p. 169.) The Greek word *logos* denotes "meaning," and logotherapy is based on the concept that striving for meaning in one's life is the primary motivational force in human beings. Hence Frankl speaks of a *will-to-meaning* in contrast to the pleasure principle (or, as he would term it, the *will-to-pleasure*) on which Freudian psychology is centered, as well as in contrast to the *will-to-power* stressed by Adlerian psychology.[12] In psychoanalysis, patients must tell their therapist things that are sometimes difficult to tell, but in logotherapy patients must hear things that are sometimes disagreeable to hear.

In our use of logotherapy we aimed at breaking up the typical self-centeredness of addicts instead of fostering and reinforcing it, as is the usual practice. We focused on assignments and meanings to be fulfilled by patients in their future.

Noted theologian Paul Tillich has defined *emptiness* and *meaninglessness* as the two levels of a threatening experience of non-being which attack spiritual affirmation, emptiness being the relative threat, and meaninglessness being the absolute threat. The anxiety of meaninglessness is "anxiety about the loss of an ultimate concern of a meaning which gives meaning to all meaning." This anxiety is aroused by the loss of a spiritual center or locus and by a conscious lack of a knowledge of the meaning of existence. This loss of a spiritual center, which leads to a loss of the meaning of life, Tillich maintains, follows the loss of God in the lives of individuals:

"... The decisive event which underlies the search for meaning and despair of it in the twentieth century is the loss of God in the nineteenth century. Feuerbach explained God away in terms of the infinite desire of the human heart; Marx explained him away in terms of an ideological attempt to rise above the given reality; Nietzsche as a weakening of the will to live. The result is the pronouncement: 'God is dead,' and with him the whole system in which one lived."[13]

Ever since the institutional churches opted out of their social and political responsibilities in the seventeenth century, followed by the end of ecclesiastical paternalism in the nineteenth century, Western society has lost its "spiritual center," and has found no spiritual corpus to replace it. In the past twenty years alone, Britain has imported nearly one hundred so-called religions—mainly from America, India, and the Far East—and, according to one newspaper report, "some are entirely innocent, some are fads, some are confidence tricks, some are products of eccentrics; a few are sinister." To paraphrase G. K. Chesterton: When a person or nation gives up belief in one God they do not believe in no gods but in any gods.

For where there is no chemical addiction—and often where there is— there is behavioral addiction in an attempt to fill the emptiness and meaninglessness in the individual and society. There is the ludicrous but sinister Unification Church of South Korea, better known as the Moonies. There was the crypto-Communist People's Temple of megalomaniac Jim Jones, which posed as a Christian organization to tap the moneyed sources of jaded Christianity in America while extorting money from its poor members in order to set up a Marxist commune in Guyana, with the whole affair ending in a holocaust of suicide and notoriety. There was the subtle and intimidating drug-rehabilitation organization of Synanon, founded by ex-alcoholic Charles Dederich, with no known "spiritual center" but with "the Game," an empirical individualist philosophy in which members denounced each other in order to work off their hostilities and gain meaningful relationships. There are the Children of God, with their notorious reputation of sexual enticement as "hookers for Jesus" while insisting that they are the only true believers. There are the many bizarre Eastern cultic imports—Transcendental Meditation, Divine Light Mission, the sex-oriented Bhagwan Shree Rajneesh movement, and the extremist Ananda Marg. There is also of course, the Christian Pentecostal movement, actively propagating their arbitrary selection of some six "charismatic gifts," out of a Biblical availability of about thirty, and sometimes being just as cultic by definition and exclusivity as their more notorious counterparts.

Implicit in all of this ritualized obsession is a critical lack of values elsewhere in modern society—that same sickness lying at the root of the problem of addicts noted by the Council of Europe in its report—and a widespread hunger and search for values and meaning. The great deceit at the heart of the problem, however, perpetuated by twentieth century doctors, is that chemicals with power to produce an altered state of consciousness, or behavioral addictions with a similar result are an adequate substitute for the real thing. Addicts know that they are being conned, and only despair drives them from one to another as a last resort.

It is evident that in the future doctors will have to emphasize spiritual meaning and well-being as well as the medical in the treatment of sickness. This is especially true in the treatment of conditions associated with the mind, such as addictions. The Judaic-Christian concept to which so many physicians subscribe (in theory if not in practice) includes in its philosophy of salvation the undisputed principle of healing. Moses, whose brass serpent on a pole restored health to the Israelites (the symbol of medical practice to this day), and Jesus, who healed and forgave sins in the New Testament, both demonstrated this truth. Paul Tillich, in *The Meaning of Health,* also emphasized its value:

"The healing of mental illness is the most crucial proof of salvation, although mental diseases are not separated off from body and social diseases in the accounts. Healing in the sense of salvation includes the conquest of death...The clearest expression of the connection between disease and death, on the one hand, and salvation and eternal life (*not* to be confused with physical immortality), on the other hand, is the famous description of the sacramental food as a *pharmakon athanasias,* a medicine which heals from death, and overcomes exclusion from the realm of eternity...

"The concept of health cannot be defined without relation to its opposite—disease. But this is not only a matter of definition. In reality, health is not health without the essential possibility and the existential reality of disease. In this sense, health is a disease conquered, as eternally the positive is positive by conquering the negative. This is the deepest theological significance of medicine."[14]

9 THE SPIRITUAL ELEMENT IN THE TREATMENT OF ADDICTIONS

There is little doubt that the most successful forms of post-detoxification treatment of addictions are those that include a foundational spiritual emphasis in their approach. This may be seen in the work of Alcoholics Anonymous, the Salvation Army, Teen Challenge, and other, non-Christian, organizations.

The transforming of the mind

Paul of Tarsus, one of the world's great thinkers and the man most responsible for explaining the true significance of Judaic-Christian philosophy as the revealed mind of God, declared as that philosophy's most fundamental principle:

"Offer your very selves to God; a living sacrifice, dedicated and fit for his acceptance, worship offered by mind and heart. Adapt yourself no longer to the pattern of this present world, *but let your minds be remade and your whole nature thus transformed. Then you will be able to discern the will of God,* and to know what is good, acceptable and perfect..." (Romans 12: 1-3, my italics)

There, stated very clearly, are the possibility and the assurance that human nature—even the worst, as Paul affirmed elsewhere—can be transformed by the re-making of the human mind, which learns, in the process, to discern the will of God. At one stroke such a discernment eliminates the problem of emptiness and meaninglessness.

The way to the mind of God by which we each may know his will for ourselves, is found by making a daily, living sacrifice of our own self-will and allowing the re-making of our own self-centered mind (which by choice and practice has been conditioned to think as "the natural mind under the spirit of this world") into a similarity to "the mind of Christ" (Christ was at all times open to the promptings of the Spirit of God regarding his ongoing purposes, and was obedient to them).

The Spirit coming from God prompts our minds, informing us what God desires for us, and evoking in us that desire—the conative impulse—to obey. As we choose to obey or to disobey, the spiritual battle begins, and is resolved as we submit our wills to the choice desired. If the choice is obedience to the mind of God, the Spirit illuminates our minds with an understanding of the commitment, and the same Spirit communicates the decision back to God. This is the process of true prayer.

William Barclay, the noted Scottish theologian, has described this word "Spirit," or "Holy Spirit," as "a word of quite special importance" and "a word of quite special difficulty." Almost all translators agree that in many instances it means "advocate;" but elsewhere it is used to mean "comforter," "helper," "someone who stands with us," or "he who is to befriend us." The word itself, *parakletos*, means literally "one who is called in," and is *passive in form*, but *active in meaning*. The Spirit is always called in to *do* something, to render some service; to help in some situation with which a person cannot cope.

It is this person in the Judaic-Christian Scriptures who delivers us from "the spirit of bondage to fear," and who brings us in the process of prayer into a new relationship and understanding of a loving heavenly Father. "The Spirit itself bears witness with our spirit that we are children of God...the Spirit also helps us in our weakness..."

Because of the presence of the Spirit we are enabled to know and become what we were created to be. Jesus himself submitted to this process when he was "led by the Spirit into the wilderness" to be tested by the Devil. There Satan used three basic principles, each active in the corruption and destruction of humankind:

(1) *the lust of the flesh:* in tempting Jesus to turn stones into bread when hungry—*pleasure* without responsibility.

(2) *the lust of the eyes:* in tempting Jesus with material possessions for personal gain—*prestige* without responsibility.

(3) *the pride of life:* tempting Jesus to do miracles for selfish reasons—*power* without responsibility.

These have always been the three basic temptations of humankind, or the three basic drives recognized by psychologists and psychiatrists in Freud's will-to-pleasure, Adler's will-to-power, and Frankl's will-to-meaning. To all of these Jesus found the answer, not in Greek myths, but in scriptural models.

The most difficult step in the transformation process—the long journey from bondage to freedom—is the first: the act of volition, the yielding of the will. The human will includes three aspects of mind: feeling, knowing and conation. We will first take the last mentioned—and least recognized—conation. The conative impulse is the initial desire or aversion which lead to a decision to act. The will comes into play when the person either checks or gives way to the impulse. The essential feature which makes the activity a willed one is that it is the person who decides whether to check the impulse or give it free play. In connection with the theological concept of sin (which means "a falling short" of God's purpose), it means not only a carrying out of wrong action but a willed consent to wrong action.

Let us return to Paul's words, then, regarding the re-making of the mind through a daily sacrifice of the self. What Paul had in mind was to be God-centered and not self-centered in all the daily decisions of life, to pause between the moment of conation and the moment of choice, and by faith choose what God wants rather than what self wants. In doing this, said Paul, "through faith...we are set free;" "through faith...we are children of God."

This is where powerlessness ends and power begins; this is where failure ends and victory begins. This is the critical point in the addicts' experience, the uncrossable hurdle, the unbridgeable gap, which—even after detoxification from the chemical of addiction—has always beaten them and left them without hope, crying out "I can't," or "it's impossible."

Faith in healing

At this point of impossibility faith, through the Spirit of God, is the cure. Faith, defined by Paul of Tarsus is "that which gives substance to our hopes, and makes us certain of realities we do not see"; faith is reaching out for the hand of God—and finding it there. And faith is a gamble; just read Paul's definition once again. It is as good a definition of gambling as can be found; the individual is putting his bet where his hopes are. But faith is also the divinely implanted instinct that enables the believer to grow in the knowledge of God. Gambling, as it has come to be known— placing of money bets for financial profit—is simply the perversion of this faith instinct into material instead of spiritual ends, just as lust is the perversion of love for physical instead of spiritual ends.

Perhaps more than any other thinker Jung has explored the inter-relationship between the physical world and the spiritual world in some thirty volumes collating evidence from his eighty years to demonstrate that the troublesome emotions of men and women cannot be healed without a radically different view of life and the world, which means taking into full consideration their contacts with the creative center of meaning.

Jung's psychology is essentially concerned with the search for wholeness, bringing together all the individual's characteristics—good and evil, conscious and unconscious—into the conscious experience of completeness and awareness. He demonstrated that the most advanced thinking supports the conviction that religion is a vitally necessary element in human life, delivering the human spirit from its bondage to a sterile materialism and a meaningless humanism.

Average men and women know little or nothing of this potential intensive or extensive consciousness, little or nothing of the spiritual certainties of their predecessors in earlier centuries (which were characterized by less material obsession and more spiritual provision). Modern ideals of material security, self-centered pursuits, vaguely-defined "good works," more leisure, pleasure-seeking, and so on, provide no adequate framework for a fulfilled or even mildly satisfying life. Those who turn away from an apparently terrifying prospect of a blind world in which there is increasing chaos, and look inward, find in their own minds even greater chaos and darkness.

But it is just there, in the recesses of the mind, that the transformation from chaos to purpose, from darkness to light, from bondage to freedom, must take place. No organic medicine has yet been found to treat neuroses successfully, no proof that psychoneuroses are glandular in nature has been discovered, but psycho-spiritual methods have been found effective, therapeutic, transforming!

Jung, commenting on the psychic factors effective in curing neuroses, has said:

"For example, a suitable explanation or a comforting word to the patient may have something like a healing effect which may even influence the glandular secretions. The doctor's words, to be sure, are 'only' vibrations in the air, yet they constitute a particular set of vibrations corresponding to a particular psychic state in the doctor. The words are effective only insofar as they convey a meaning or have significance. But meaning is something mental or spiritual. Call it a fiction if you like. None the less it enables us to influence the cause of the disease in a far more effective way than with chemical preparations. We can even influence the biochemical processes of the body by it. Whether the fiction arises in me spontaneously, or reaches me from without by way of human speech, it can make me ill or cure me... Nothing is more effective in the psychic and even psychophysical realm."[1]

Jung, while not a Christian in the orthodox sense, held strong opinions about the phenomenon of evil "since every psyche is fascinated by it," and he maintained that "the principal and indeed only thing that is wrong with the world is man." Further, he held that "...it is only the meaningful that sets us free."[2]

But for "meaning" to make a difference in the individual concerned there has to be understanding of some kind between the speaker and the listener—a state of "conditional readiness" which activates response. For example, as has been noted, a conversation fundamentally begins when a puff of air, produced by vibrations of the speaker's larynx, echoes around the cavities of his mouth and results in a characteristic sequence of soundwaves travelling through space and vibrating the sensitive membranes of the listener's ear, giving rise to nerve impulses, and so on. Where does "meaning" conveyed and received come into this process? Whether the speaker is a genius elucidating an astounding truth, or an idiot jabbering nonsense, the medium of communication is the same.

How to have a fully equipped mind
The writer of the Book of Hebrews declared that mature individuals were those "who have their faculties trained by practice to distinguish between good and evil."

The perception that leads to memory, understanding and will and eventually to wisdom is a faculty that can be trained. However, if it is never used it can atrophy and become a wasted asset, like its physical counterparts.

The Greeks, according to Dr. William Barclay, had three important words to describe the three great qualities of mind; any man or woman who had these had "a mind fully equipped." They were:

(1) *Sophia,* meaning wisdom, the ultimate knowledge of things human and divine, which is nothing less than the knowledge of God. *Sophia* represents the furthest reach of the human mind.

(2) *Phronesis,* meaning prudence. While *sophia* refers primarily to theoretical concepts, *phronesis* is practical and has to do with a person's life, conduct and action. Aristotle defined *phronesis* as "truth... concerned with action in relation to the things that are good for human beings."

(3) *Sunesis,* meaning understanding, is concerned with judgment, the reaching of a conclusion, a synthesis in the sense of "putting two and two together;" it is the power to distinguish between two separate courses of action, varying values, differing relationships between people; it refers to the ability to test, to distinguish, to evaluate and to form judgment.

In elaborating on these three great qualities of mind, Dr. Barclay comments:

"There is clearly growth in wisdom. Although wisdom is not the discovery of the mind, it cannot be obtained without the strenuous activity of the mind. Real wisdom comes when the Spirit of God reaches down to meet the searching mind of man, but the mind of man must search before God will come to meet it. Wisdom is not for the mentally lazy, although it is a gift of God..."[3]

Wisdom is acquired when the thing known is put to its proper use. Understanding is knowing what is that proper use.

That chemicals should be able to provide essential wisdom and understanding, as Dr. Timothy Leary stated during the late 1960s and early 1970s, is ludicrous. Arthur Koestler put it very well:

"...It is fundamentally wrong, and naive, to expect that drugs can present the mind with gratis gifts—put into it something which is not already there. Neither mystic insights, nor philosophic wisdom, nor creative power, can be provided by pill or injection. The psychopharmacist cannot *add* to the faculties of the brain—but he can, at best, *eliminate* obstructions and blockages which impede their proper use. He cannot aggrandize us—but he can, within limits, normalize us; he cannot put additional circuits within the brain, but he can, again within limits, improve the coordination between existing ones, attenuate conflicts, prevent the blowing of fuses, and ensure a steady power supply. That is all the help we can ask for—but if we were able to attain it, the benefits for mankind would be incalculable. . ."[4]

One of the most intriguing questions being thrown up by the discovery of endorphins is the possible part they play in the behavior of the "cult-addict" as well as the "chemical-addict," the "object-addict," and the "person-addict." The question is this: does the person who becomes cult, object, or person-addicted also diminish the production of natural endorphins required to meet life's challenges and the stresses of pain and emotion; and then, under the new stimulus of another cult, object, or person, does the body again respond temporarily—until that new addiction in turn is proved inadequate to the individual's current situation? If so, this theory would go a long way towards explaining why genuine "spiritual healing" can suddenly and dramatically "cure" individual and group addiction through *intense belief operating as an electrical stimulus for the manufacture and release of endorphins,* while minor cultic fads are usually successful only for short periods because of their superficial character.

These observations arose out of our increasing involvement with patients from different nations, cultures, religions, and backgrounds. Why does Hong Kong, with four million Chinese, have the worst drug addiction problem in the world, while mainland China across the border, with almost one billion Chinese, apparently has none? Why did Chinese Maoism produce no chemical addictions while Soviet Marxism struggles with a monumental alcoholism problem? Why is Buddhist meditation so successful in Thailand, with almost a million heroin addicts (that is, when they can get addicts detoxified enough to meditate)? Why does an authoritarian and ascetic religion like Islam have so many heroin and alcohol addicts in areas such as Indonesia and Iran? Why is it, that when the environment is changed—politically, culturally, socially, spiritually—there is a direct and often dramatic effect on what had appeared to be the insoluble problem of addictions? In all the questions, the solutions treated seriously the negative factors of emptiness and meaninglessness and their removal, and the positive factors of vision, values, and some form of adequate and applied belief system for individuals and nations.

The real cure for addiction

The cure for addiction, like the cure for tuberculosis, involves fundamental changes in society. For tuberculosis to be removed as a medical and social scourge, more than medication and surgery were required; a new political and social approach to housing, hygiene, and diet was needed as well.

Addiction is also a social disease, though much more complex and pernicious than tuberculosis. After medication, the re-structuring of family, community, social, political, and ecclesiastical values and patterns are essential. The real cure for addiction requires revolution—spiritual revolution.

A recent authoritative article in the *New England Journal of Medicine* on the subject of the serious, widespread abuse of mind-altering drugs in the U.S.A., sub-titled "A Modern Epidemic," declared:

"What motivates such a vast segment of our society to inhale, ingest, or inject into our bodies this wide assortment of mind-altering substances? When asked this question, those who reported using marijuana daily said that they did so primarily to alter how they felt—to help cope with feelings of stress, anger, depression, frustration, or boredom. College students who used LSD said they took the drug to reduce feelings of loneliness and isolation, to enhance creativity and productiveness, to increase social and sexual effectiveness, and to fill a 'moral and spiritual void.' In essence, people take these drugs to alter or escape from a less than tolerable society, and to meet intense emotional needs...

"In addition, a vast body of research has shown that the absence of a parent through death, divorce or a time-demanding job contributes to many forms of emotional disorder, especially the anger, rebelliousness, low self-esteem, depression, and anti-social behavior that characterize drug users. Changes in child-rearing practices and family stability in the United States, beginning several years before the drug culture evolved, have shifted child care from parents to other agencies. Cross-cultural studies indicate that American parents spend less time with their children than parents in any other nation in the world except England. The accelerating divorce rate in the United States has closely paralleled the rise in drug use, and over half the children under the age of 18 (approximately 13 million) live in a home with one or both parents missing. Moreover poor academic performance, susceptibility to peer influence, and delinquent behavior (all characteristic of drug users), as well as suicide and homicide, have been found to be more pronounced among children from homes with one or both parents missing or frequently absent..."[5]

The need for spiritual revolution of society is also Alexandr Solzhenitsyn's prophetic message to the West in a different context. As he argues in his books and broadcasts, spiritual solutions to society's problems, and the discarding of useless materialist substitutes now being promulgated, result from true Christian freedom. This is very different from the unlimited freedom of the Western ideal and the Marxist concept of freedom as acceptance of the yoke of necessity; Christian freedom is *self-restriction.* Discipline of the self for the sake of others. In Solzhenitsyn's words:

"Once understood and adopted, this principle diverts us—as individuals, in all forms of association, societies and nations—from *outward* to *inward* development, thereby giving us greater spiritual depth.

"The turn toward *inward* development, the triumph of inwardness over outwardness, if it ever happens, will be a great turning point in the history of mankind, comparable to the transition from the Middle Ages to the Renaissance. There will be a complete change not only in the direction of our interests and activities but in the very nature of human beings (a change from spiritual dispersal to spiritual concentration), and a greater change still in the character of human societies. If in some places this is destined to be a revolutionary process, these revolutions will not be like earlier ones—physical, bloody and never beneficial—but will be *moral revolutions,* requiring both courage and sacrifice, though not cruelty—a new phenomenon in human history, of which little is yet known and which as yet no one has prophetically described in clear and precise forms."[6]

While I was researching chemical addictions and electrical stimulation, my husband, George, was pursuing research into these philosophical aspects of the problems of behavioral addictions. The variety of patients that we had, with their own complex background of experiences and forms of treatment, provided a fascinating spectrum for investigation—to them as well as to us. We had patients from Iran and Lebanon, Spain and Italy, Germany and France, Argentina and Brazil, of all classes and creeds, and out of our experience with them we worked out, by trial and error, a system of treatment which could be used for both detoxification and rehabilitation in the clinic we were preparing for our clinical trials.

PART III
TREATING
ADDICTIONS

10 THE PHARMAKON CLINIC AND MARIE CURIE RESEARCH

The airing of the second BBC television documentary, "Still Off The Hook," in July 1977, provided me with several unexpected opportunities. The film had featured the same drug addict as in the first film, "Off the Hook." Two years after his treatment by NET, he was still off his drugs, looking well, and working in the same part of London as before, where drugs were easily available. The second film concluded with a segment filmed in the United States, in which Dr. Corbett, one of the American doctors involved in the treatment of Keith Richards, was interviewed about his conclusions regarding NET. He said he was so impressed with its results that he was trying to persuade the U.S. authorities to invite me to the United States.

The positive public reaction to the showing of this second BBC film produced three offers of funding for research, the most important of which was from The Rank Foundation. This foundation offered to provide premises and finance for one year's clinical trial in a unit which would reflect my fundamental theories regarding both detoxification[1] and rehabilitation.[2]

At first I had thought of concentrating on detoxification and then sending the detoxified patients to therapeutic centers for rehabilitation. But it became quickly apparent that there were very few therapeutic centers with vacancies available. Consequently, I drew up a program, with my husband George as Director of Counselling, which provided for ten days of detoxification, followed by up to thirty days of rehabilitation.

The Pharmakon Clinic

The manor house in which the first clinic was set up could accommodate twenty-five patients in shared or single rooms and had a large lounge, dining room, and recreation room for common use. For recreation, various games were available in the lounge, and tennis, croquet, swimming, and fishing on the grounds. It was anticipated that most patients would stay up to forty days, with the focus of the first ten days being primarily on detoxification, followed by a month of counseling to help the detoxified individuals find new meaning in life. It was hoped that such counseling would enable them to reenter society as whole persons with the capacity to function adequately without drugs. In 1980 the cost of the forty day stay was about $2,000.

Besides myself as senior medical consultant, the medical staff included one other doctor, a nursing supervisor and the equivalent of eleven full-time nurses. My husband had a number of counselors on his staff and we had an administrator, secretary, and other individuals in charge of housekeeping, cooking, gardening, and maintenance, for a total staff of about twenty-five. The professional staff participated in regular training courses in NET and in specialized counseling courses, as appropriate. Group meetings of staff members were held to evaluate the progress of each patient's therapy. My husband and I and our three children lived in the manor house and ate our meals with the patients and staff every day. We considered our observable interaction with each other as a family, and the patients' interaction with a normal family and caring counselors, to be an important part of the therapeutic process.

The clinic was designed to treat all types of chemical or behavioral dependencies and addictions, associated neural conditions, and chronic pain. Residents could be accepted while on probation, direct from prison, or while on trial if circumstances warranted. For the residence program we could accept employed persons only if they could obtain at least ten days' leave for the first phase of the program. We were prepared to consider couples, under special circumstances, or minors, with parental consent. We did not accept frankly psychotic or schizophrenic patients, and could not at that time accept patients with severe physical disabilities. Patients who left without permission were not readmitted without a multidisciplinary discussion of the reasons for their departure. As we said in our official descriptive literature about the clinic, however, "No patient will be left without hope of treatment."

Admission procedures could be initiated by the individual or his or her physician, or by any other relevant individual or agency, by telephone or letter. Reports on the individual's history or condition were considered useful but not essential at the time of initial assessment by the senior medical consultant. Applicants were given leaflets or pamphlets describing Pharmakon Clinic, its ground rules, and both the nature and philosophy of our treatment.

Referral agencies or immediate relatives were invited to visit the clinic to see it for themselves before the selection interview. Although the patient's motivation was not an essential factor for acceptance, it did influence our decision about an admission date.

The program

Residents do not have to be drug-free when admitted, but the only drugs given after admission are for existing medical conditions (if any) or for any illness that might occur during the treatment period. Because ground rules are designed to prevent a return to the addiction, visiting, telephoning, and correspondence are allowed only rarely, at the discretion of the senior medical consultant or counselor.

No patient is allowed beyond the grounds of the estate unaccompanied during the initial treatment period, and patients are warned that any evidence of drug-taking will result in their immediate discharge. Cigarette smoking is restricted to certain areas. Generally, residents are expected to be up at 7 A.M. on weekdays and 8:30 A.M. on Sundays, to keep their rooms orderly, and to maintain a neat and clean personal appearance. As part of their therapy, but not as a duty, they are asked to assist with various domestic tasks.

For the first six days, NET stimulation is given day and night and patients are encouraged to take outdoor exercise in the large grounds and to begin some recreation. Appropriate household duties are assigned from the start. As detoxification takes effect, NET is diminished accordingly and counseling, mostly individual but also in groups, is gradually increased up until the tenth day. Then begins a further thirty-day period of rehabilitation specifically planned for each patient's needs. At this stage, family and/or spouse are always requested to participate in counseling for themselves as well as for the patient.

One of the problems with the rapid detoxification produced by NET is that patients are suddenly faced again with all the problems that led to addiction. On the fourth day, experienced addicts know that if they haven't had any withdrawal symptoms, they aren't going to have any. With their own enkephalin flooding their systems once again, they generally experience an immense euphoria, thinking "At last I've got this thing licked."

But as my husband described in an interview in *Radix* magazine, "The fourth day is a sixteen-hour one, starting at 8 o'clock in the morning and going right through to 10 or 12 o'clock at night. The addicts have to look at themselves as they have not looked at themselves in years. They are facing a day in which they don't have to try to con husband, wife, or friend. They don't have to rip off the police or a gas station or pharmacy. They are just sitting, and that hurts. They've gotten out of the habit of filling their days with anything constructive, whether it's working, reading, listening to music, or whatever. They have sixteen hours of total boredom, in which they are left looking at the problem that they looked at the day they started on drugs. They didn't like themselves back then, they didn't like their lives, parents, home, society, church, or God. But they managed to live with all those things as long as they had the chemical. Now that their chemical has been taken away they are brought back to the day in which they first decided to run from their problems."[3]

Thus the second phase of the Pharmakon Treatment is designed to help individuals who are, on the one hand, full of hope that they can overcome addiction, but who are at the same time becoming aware of their own total inadequacy in dealing with personal, psychological, social, domestic, or spiritual problems.

We begin every morning by having them spend an hour looking at a newspaper, or reading and thinking about some other material such as the Bible, Gibran's *The Prophet,* or even Karl Marx, if they choose that. The idea is to begin feeding and exercising their minds with tasks of gradually increasing challenge, especially where their mental faculties had been badly eroded by long-term use of drugs.

This is followed by therapy in the form of nonrecreational work activities and talks with doctors and counsellor. The afternoons are for recreational therapy such as tennis, swimming, or games, plus individual and group therapy sessions.

No arrangements are made for the employment of patients during a short-term stay, but a list of possible employers and training programs is prepared for later use.

Residents are encouraged to maintain regular contact with the clinic staff following the completion of their in-patient rehabilitation, and a list of families, support groups, churches, and other interested agencies nationwide provides continuing support for former patients. A counselling information package is available to send to all interested employers with their own medical welfare plans.

The Pharmakon philosophy

Believing that addiction has a physiological as well as a psychological derivation, and that the latter, to a great extent, is caused by lack of meaningful relationship with family, relatives, community, or God, and of an inadequate experiential framework to cope with the chosen environment, the Pharmakon philosophy is to treat the whole person, body, mind and spirit, so that not only the chemical or behavioral addiction is cured, but also the underlying cause which produced the addiction in the first place.

The Pharmakon Clinic is not a religious organization. It has treated Muslims, Buddhists, Marxists, and Hindus as well as Christians, agnostics, and atheists who seek freedom from chemical and behavioral addictions. But it is staffed by personnel who have a wholesome commitment to spiritual ideas and who are professionals, with acknowledged expertise in their fields. There are no psychiatrists on the resident or consultant staff, since addiction is believed to be fundamentally a spiritual problem requiring spiritual solutions which can be more than adequately provided by trained paraprofessionals with a knowledge and experience of addictions and spiritual values.

Success defined

We are satisfied that rehabilitation is complete when the patient is healed in body, mind, and spirit, and has comprehended and shown a capacity to apply a new philosophy of life appropriate to his or her chosen environment. No longer in bondage to a chemical or behavioral addiction, former addicts can live a life with freedom, joy, and love within the family and community. Not many have fully met the above criteria, but 90 percent are at various stages along the way, with real hope—which is as much as any of us have.

Research at the Marie Curie Laboratories

While the Pharmakon Clinic trial was going ahead I was also deeply involved in the research at the Marie Curie Memorial Foundation Research Laboratories, investigating the biochemical basis of NET. This had been made possible by further financial aid from the rock music world, this time from Pete Townshend and The Who, which had a reputation for being "the greatest rock-and-roll group in the world."

Pete had come regularly to visit Eric Clapton while I was treating him, and had been so impressed with what NET had done for Eric that he had volunteered to help in any way possible. He and the other members of The Who conducted a series of concerts and donated a large part of the proceeds towards my research.

My colleague at the Marie Curie Research Laboratories, Dr. Ifor Capel, was very enthusiastic when he saw the initial responses from our investigations. Interest in my work on the part of the Marie Curie scientists stemmed from their cancer research and their desire to investigate the biological basis and effects of NET in cancer conditions related to alcohol and nicotine. In the first investigations, however, they saw NET's dramatic effect in ameliorating restraint stress in rats. They found that plasma levels of the adrenal hormone cortisol, which is an indicator of stress, were significantly lower in the NET-treated rats than in the control animals.[4]

Since stress is considered to play an important part in the onset of cancer, the optimistic results of NET were of great interest to the Marie Curie researchers, and they expanded their investigations into other areas.

Our research over a four year period had expanded our knowledge of the modus operandi of NET. It had also confirmed that the various parameters of current which I had discovered by trial and error over the previous several years to be optimum in treating patients, were in most cases the same parameters found to be optimum in detoxifying rats from various drugs, in a series of controlled experiments. Rapid detoxification was a consistent finding in all the rat experiments throughout the four years, *provided the correct parameters were used.*[5,6,7]

It is well known that alcohol abuse damages the liver; it is less well known that many drug abusers, even those who have never contracted hepatitis, also have damaged livers. After NET treatment, liver function improved rapidly in patients with hepatic insufficiency. We also demonstrated in rats that hepatic enzyme activity is enhanced by NET;[4] and, in healthy humans, hepatic efficiency improved (unpublished observations). And as Dr. Robert Moore expressed it, "Detoxification of alcohol is a function of the liver, not doctors or hospitals or detoxification centers."[8]

Other researchers have reported a controlled trial showing that endorphin levels are markedly lower in heroin addicts than in healthy subjects, presumably because the opioid receptors are constantly occupied by the exogenous heroin causing a feed-back suppression of the endorphin-producing system."[9] Also, deficient ACTH production has been found in methadone addicts, with "subsequent secondary hypoadrenalism," (some researchers claim it is a primary hypoadrenalism[10]) which could explain their "fatiguability, weakness, anorexia, weight loss, depression and gastrointestinal dysfunction" which "often persist long after detoxification and are commonly associated with recidivism."[11] NET has now been demonstrated to increase not only serum endorphin levels in rats and humans (unpublished observations) but it can also increase serum "corticosterone levels *when the appropriate current is used.*"[6] This latter effect may explain the impressively rapid elimination of the long-term lethargy and other symptoms mentioned above, after only ten day's treatment by NET.

Other medical benefits of NET

In an investigation of the effects of NET on the terminal pain of cancer, thirty patients with widespread bone tumors throughout their bodies were studied. Although they were suffering severe pain, all thirty patients stated that NET was either as good as or better than their usual large dose of morphine. NET also prevented any withdrawal symptoms from the morphine dependency.

Again, our work with the Marie Curie scientists showed increased levels of the neurotransmitter serotonin in rats[5] and humans (unpublished observations), while receiving NET. This is a possible mechanism for the mood elevation observed after changing to the correct current frequency when an addict experiences depression during the withdrawal period. It has been shown that chronic alcoholics, during a phase of abstinence, have reduced serotonin; that many patients suffering from depression have low levels of serotonin; and that the risk of suicide is greater in those with low serotonin levels.[12] It has also been suggested that serotonin deficiencies may be a factor in obesity though the possible effect of NET in this area has yet to be investigated.

Over forty neurotransmitters have now been discovered.[13] While altered measurements of these substances in any disease or through NET are very significant, it is often difficult to know if the change is cause, or effect, or merely part of a chain reaction. However, stimulation of hormone and neurotransmitter production appears to be just as dependent on the correct choice of current parameters as it is in detoxification from substance abuse. I am continuing to research these mechanisms in the U.S.A.

Meanwhile, the results of the effects of NET in stress were important and encouraging to me, first, because they confirmed my own clinical findings with NET over the years, and also because of the scale of the stress problem world-wide and the significant part it played in addictions and other diseases. According to Dr. Hans Selye, an endocrinologist known for his pioneering studies of the effects of stress on the human body, even such illnesses as arthritis, heart disease, kidney disease and other circulatory disturbances can often be traced to an overproduction of adrenal hormones due to stress.

"The apparent cause of illness," he stated, "is often an infection, an intoxication, nervous exhaustion, or merely old age, but actually a breakdown of the hormonal mechanism seems to be the most ultimate cause of death in man...People could live past 100 by understanding and conquering stress, by taking it into our hands and examining its clinical and psychological properties. Stress has got such properties, and they can be measured."[14]

From the preliminary results of our research, therefore, it appeared that with the successful achievement of addiction detoxification we might be opening the door to a revolutionary approach to treatment for other hitherto intractable human diseases.

11 THE PHARMAKON CLINIC TREATMENT

Strictly speaking, the Pharmakon Clinic Treatment was only peripherally concerned with what is usually meant by "rehabilitation." Our primary concern and emphasis was on "transformation."

Rehabilitation is normally associated with restoring individuals to what they were before the onset of illness or a deteriorating physical condition. But the Pharmakon Treatment was directed towards transforming individuals whose inadequacies had made them, or had contributed towards their becoming, addicts in the first place; it showed them how to become new men and women.

Here I will repeat an excerpt from the writing of Peter Lawrie, already used in an earlier chapter, in order to refresh the reader's memory as to the uniqueness of the problem of treating addicts of all kinds. The treatment of addiction is unlike the treatment of any other condition, as I have tried to show in preceding chapters. The problem has obscure and complex psycho-spiritual roots embedded deeply in family and social relationships. Consequently, the solution must reach down to those deep roots by radical psychospiritual means in much the same way that radical surgery must deeply and cleanly deal with a malignancy.

In *Drugs: Medical, Psychological and Social Facts,* Peter Lawrie has accurately described the therapeutic problem:

"Addicts are notoriously resistant to ordinary psychotherapy. One way of looking at this is to observe that analysis depends on communication, on the patient's acceptance of the therapist as a real human being who can have a real effect on him. But the addict's whole life is organised to remove any dependence on humanity; given his drugs he is self-sufficient, able to generate his own satisfactions and guilts and to live a rich emotional life independent of the outside world. He therefore has no motives for communication when things are going well; when he does present himself for treatment it is often not because he wants to be cured of addiction, but because his addiction is not working as it should. *He is a two-time loser who wants to get back to being a one-time loser, not to take the much more perilous step to being an unloser.* The ordinary psychiatric patient is like a burr, offering many hooks to the world and the therapist—often too many; the therapist's best strategy is to stand still and let his patient attach himself as he will. But the addict is like a nut: smooth and with a thick armour. The only hook he offers is his need for drugs, and that can be satisfied in a number of ways. *To reach the addict, his shell must be cracked.* We might guess that it would be necessary to counter the coercion of opiates with the coercion of therapy..."[1] (my italics)

Mission: to confront and convince

If the goal of the Pharmakon Clinic Treatment was *transformation,* the starting point was *confrontation.* This was not an artificial process derived from the necessity of "cracking the nut" of the addict, but a spiritual principle described by Jesus Christ, who taught that self-centered individuals who arrogantly alienate themselves from God and others must be halted and turned round; that the self-will must be recognized, admitted, repented of, rejected, and replaced by the forgiveness and love of God; and that this experience will transform the most depraved individuals and deliver them from their bondage.

Jesus taught that the Spirit's work was to convict of sin, and righteousness, and judgment, to guide our minds into all truth, to proclaim things that are to come, and to reveal the mind of God. "You shall know the truth," declared Jesus, "and the truth shall make you free."

Thus the basis of the Pharmakon Treatment "confrontation therapy" is that counseling requires *convicting* and *convincing* before the *transforming* of the mind could take place.

Biblical models

In our comprehensive application, analysis and advice were supplied not on the usual pattern of Greek myths but on Biblical models. For example, the merciful and loving father of Jesus in Luke 15 is presented rather than the self-centered and murderous son of Freud's Oedipus. The psychotherapeutic orientation of the Pharmakon Treatment could be loosely described as Frankl-Jungian in general and Judaic-Christian in particular. That is, it agrees with Jung's statement:

"During the past thirty years people from all over the civilized countries on earth have consulted me... Among all my patients in the second half of life—that is to say, over thirty-five—there has not been one whose problem in the last resort was not that of finding a religious outlook on life. It is safe to say that every one of them felt ill because he had lost that which the living religions of every age have given to their followers, and none of them has been really healed who did not regain his religious outlook..."

And again:

"...A psycho-neurosis must be understood as the suffering of a human being who has not discovered what life means for him. All creativeness in the life of the spirit arises from a state of mental suffering..."[2]

It was this extra spiritual dimension, primarily in a Judaic-Christian context (although every patient was encouraged in the free choice of a belief system) which Pharmakon Treatment sought to provide.

Seeing the real world

In using logotherapy Frankl emphasized that the logotherapist is neither a teacher nor preacher. If he or she has a personal belief system it is for that individual alone and for the interested individual who asks about it. Changing the metaphor, the logotherapist is not a painter but an eye specialist. A painter paints the world as he or she sees it; the eye specialist enables the individual to see the world as it is.

The world as it is is not merely an expression of one's self; nor is it a vehicle or instrument to give one's self significance or meaning. The world is the place, or the combination of circumstances and experiences, within which one aspect of human existence and meaning is to be found; the other aspect is found within men and women who live in that world, in their own psyche.

That is why so-called "self-actualization" will never succeed in providing satisfaction or meaning; it is only half the solution. The full solution lies in self-transcendence, of which self-actualization is but the side-effect.

Like sex without love, self-actualization without self-transcendence leads to satiety and not to satisfaction.

Three paths to meaning
According to logotherapy, therefore, the meaning of life can be discovered in three different ways: one, by doing a deed; two, by experiencing a value; three, by suffering. The first is found in *the accomplishment of a set task.* The second, by *experiencing truth*—beauty, mercy, justice, right-doing, (for example; in loving a person—lover, spouse, or neighbor—as one's self). The third way to find meaning is by *suffering;* by seeking and finding the lesson in some trial or crisis experience; understanding, absorbing, and profiting from it; working through it, sharing it with others, and growing because of it.

A profound and challenging example of this was Dr. Frankl's own experience in facing the ultimate horror in the twentieth century—the gas chamber holocaust of Auschwitz:

"Let me recall that which was perhaps the deepest experience I had in the concentration camp. The odds of surviving the camp were no more than one to twenty-eight, as can be verified by exact statistics. It did not even seem possible, let alone probable, that the manuscript of my first book, which I had hidden in my coat when I arrived at Auschwitz, would ever be rescued. Thus, I had to undergo and to overcome the loss of my spiritual child. And now it seemed as if nothing and no one would survive me; neither a physical nor a spiritual child of my own! So I found myself confronted with the question of whether under such circumstances my life was ultimately void of any meaning.

"Not yet did I notice that an answer to this question with which I was wrestling so passionately was already in store for me, and that soon thereafter this answer would be given to me. This was the case when I had to surrender my clothes and in turn inherited the worn-out rags of an inmate who had been sent to the gas chamber immediately after his arrival at the Auschwitz railway station. Instead of the many pages of my manuscript, I found in the pocket of the newly acquired coat a single page torn out of a Hebrew prayer book, which contained the main Jewish prayer, *Shema Yisrael.* How should I have interpreted such a 'coincidence' other than as a challenge to *live* my thoughts instead of merely putting them on paper?

"A bit later, I remember, it seemed to me that I would die in the near future. In this critical situation, however, my concern was different from that of most of my comrades. Their question was, 'Will we survive the camp? For, if not, all this suffering has no meaning.' The question which beset me was 'Has all this suffering, this dying around us, a meaning? For, if not, then ultimately there is no meaning to survival; for a life whose meaning depends on such a happenstance—whether one escapes or not— ultimately would not be worth living at all.' "[3] (See Appendix XVI, p. 172.)

The Pharmakon Treatment was based on the conviction that life held an ultimate meaning and that this was knowable by any individual who was prepared to seek it out. The goal of the Treatment was to provide the individual with a compass with which to begin a new journey, and to let him or her experience the excitement of discovering a new world of which he or she was a meaningful part. In the words of poet Christopher Fry:

> *"Thank God our time is now, when wrong*
> *Comes up to meet us everywhere*
> *Never to leave us till we take*
> *The longest stride of soul man ever took—*
> *Affairs are now soul size*
> *The enterprise*
> *Is exploration into God."*

The new framework

Patients were encouraged to look at their chosen environment from a different viewpoint, with a different set of values, which would instil meaning instead of despair, enabling them to break out of the prison of self-interest, the monomania of "me first" and "me only," which had brought them to where they were. Our goal was to provide them with a framework of knowledge "adequate to the thing to be known," or, more precisely, adequate to their chosen environment (for which they were responsible) in order to cure the underlying emptiness and meaninglessness resulting from a previous lack of adequate values.

Obviously, in the short time spent at the Clinic it was not possible to provide a complete philosophy of life for every patient. But keeping in mind that our goal was only to give patients a compass, let me give an example of our approach.

Imagine a person who has a fear of water, and cannot swim. To give him a philosophy to explain fear, or an explanation of Archimedes' principle, or the formula for the constituent elements of water, or all of these plus a theology of God as Creator, would be useless. Instead, you must teach him how to dog paddle by getting into the water with him, supporting his chin, getting his hands and legs moving, then standing back as he begins to swim on his own. At that point the fear goes, and enjoyment starts—and he becomes receptive to this new mode of progress. Next, he wants to swim the length of the pool, then to learn the crawl and backstroke. He is eager to sail a boat, a yacht, and to venture out on the ocean instead of being content with quiet harbor sailing. He learns about currents and winds and stars. He has accepted a new philosophy of life—and all because he learned to dog paddle.

In the time at the Clinic, therefore, the aim was to uncover the patients' basic problems, find solutions based on values related to a philosophy of life; and when the patients saw it working, launch them with confidence and even enjoyment in the world that had formerly defeated them. It had worked for us; why should it not work for them? Was their basic problem bitterness against a father, or mother, or wife, or husband? Then get the parent or spouse to come to the Clinic, discuss the problem separately, then together, and get both parties to begin to practice love and forgiveness instead of hate and resentment. Try it for a week or a month. Try it with a written contract or a verbal agreement, if necessary, to overcome doubt and skepticism. But *try* it. Don't just speculate about it. Don't just theorize. *Act* on the basis of those values, expressing responses of love instead of responses of hate, practicing forgiveness, when there were lapses, instead of recrimination and resentment. And it worked.

The cure of addiction, as with the cure of emptiness and meaninglessness for whatever reason, requires not only a spiritual point of departure—an assumption that the spiritual is an essential part of human nature—but also a spiritual center around which all activity revolves, and a spiritual goal towards which the individual progresses. It is this spiritual orientation which gives meaning to life.

Psychoanalysis vs. logotherapy

In psychoanalysis the emphasis is retrospective and introspective; but in logotherapy the focus is on the assignments and meanings to be fulfilled by the patients in their future. In psychoanalysis the typical and chronic self-centeredness is reinforced and fostered; but in logotherapy it is broken up and turned outwards as illustrated above. Logotherapy is what is known as "existential psychiatry," and in existential analysis one does *not* dictate what a person should be responsible for: the realization of certain values, the fulfilment of certain tasks, the particular meaning to life. But it does consist in bringing the individuals to the point where they can freely discern their own proper tasks, out of the consciousness of their own responsibilities, and can find the clear, unique meaning of their own lives. In meeting the challenge to respond, each person accepts the responsibility.

Logotherapy, therefore, ultimately educates a person towards accepting responsibility. Blind response to a stimulus is what happens to animals—*vide* Pavlov's salivating dogs—but acceptance of responsibility can only be undertaken properly by those who understand the implications of the response stimulus.

The addict is a confident and experienced liar whose obsession with self-indulgence has forced him to lie to parents, to spouse, to children, to employer, to police, to doctor, to pharmacists, to fellow-addicts, to family, to friends, to relatives, in a widening web of deceit that feeds on the measure of its success.

This has been described by one experienced writer:

"His (the addict's) conception of himself is that of a fairly worthless creature who can hardly move about in society without a constant barrage of anxiety. (With drugs) he leaves the world of symbolic interaction behind in one fundamental sense; for although he may continue to function as a medical practitioner, a musician, etc., he is no longer dependent on it for his sense of self-value."[4]

The Pharmakon Treatment was built around Frankl's *four basic symptoms*,[3] and Jung's *four basic faculties*.[5] Frankl defines collective neurosis as comprising four basic symptoms: (1) a planless, goalless, day-to-day attitude towards life, (2) a fatalistic attitude toward life, (3) collective thinking, or abandonment of free and responsible decisions; and (4) fanaticism, or blind following of self-opinion. (It was George Santayana who said: "Fanaticism consists of redoubling your effort when you have forgotten your aim.") All of these lead to "the pathological spirit of our time as a mental epidemic." These four symptoms are characteristically recognizable to anyone who works with drug addicts and alcoholics.

But, Frankl continues, as long as man is capable of conflict of conscience he will be immune to fanaticism and to collective neuroses in general. Conversely, one who suffers from collective neurosis will overcome it if he or she is enabled once more to hear the voice of conscience, and suffer from it: "Ultimately, all of these four symptoms can be traced back to man's fear of responsibility and his escape from freedom. Yet responsibility and freedom comprise the spiritual domain of man."[3]

Carl Jung saw human beings as possessing four basic faculties: sensation, thinking, feeling, and intuition. Some people have more of one than another, but everyone needs a balance of all four "faculties" to be a healthy human being. The four faculties correspond to the obvious means by which consciousness obtains its orientation to experience.

Jung went on to define the four faculties: *sensation* (or sense perception) which tells us that something exists; *thinking,* which tells us what it is; *feeling,* which tells us whether it is agreeable or not; and *intuition,* which tells us where it comes from and where it is going. When those four basic faculties are not in proper balance, "disorders" occur, thrusting the individual into doubt and uncertainty, the twin pillars that reinforce anxiety, stress, and drugs.

Returning to Frankl who believed that "being human means being conscious and being responsible," we also note the characteristics of healthy human existence he specified: (1) education in responsibility; (2) education in freedom to decide; and (3) education in spirituality. These three characteristics are necessary to combat emptiness and meaninglessness.

The gap between the three factors which characterize healthy human existence and the four basic symptoms of despair over meaninglessness is the gap which must be bridged through the four faculties listed by Jung, as diagrammed below:

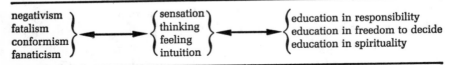

| negativism fatalism conformism fanaticism | sensation thinking feeling intuition | education in responsibility education in freedom to decide education in spirituality |

Figure 4

True freedom with responsibility—the goal

The purpose of the Pharmakon Treatment process is to help patients understand the meaning of freedom and responsibility and apply them in life. Frankl states that "in the end, education must be education towards the ability to decide," and that what is presented for decision must not only be a comprehensive and relative "framework of meaning," but also leave the individual with the knowledge of ultimate responsibility and freedom to choose acceptance or rejection.

Freedom is a relative term in any language, philosophy or religion. Jean Jacques Rousseau declared: "Man is born free, but he is everywhere in chains." Socrates said: "How can you call a man free when his pleasures rule over him"? We quote again what Solzhenitsyn has written in our own day:

"Save through self-restriction there is no other true freedom for mankind. After the Western ideal of unlimited freedom, after the Marxist concept of freedom as acceptance of the yoke of necessity—here is the true Christian concept of freedom. Freedom is *self-restriction!* Restriction of the self for the sake of others!

"Once understood and adapted, this principle diverts us—as individuals, in all forms of human associations, societies and nations—from *outward* to *inward* development, thereby giving us greater spiritual depth..."[6]

Solzhenitsyn's definition of freedom parallels that of India's sage-philosopher-poet, Rabindrinath Tagore, who wrote: "Freedom from the bondage of the soil is no liberty for the tree."

It is this concept of freedom—which Solzhenitsyn goes on to describe as "a revolutionary turning point in the history of mankind, comparable to the transition from the Middle Ages to the Renaissance"—that has its unique origins in the Judaic-Christian Scriptures which have moulded so many of Western civilization's ideals. It involves freely forsaking the bondage to self, and willingly accepting the bondage to God. As Bob Dylan sings: "You gotta serve somebody."

Recognizing truth

Regarding the significant place of truth in deliverance from self-bondage, it is worth repeating once more what Jesus declared: "If you continue in my words, then are you my disciples indeed: and you shall know the truth, and the truth shall make you free."

Jesus was not just declaring a principle of universal value, important as that would be (for the observance of a recognized standard of truth in personal, group, national, and international relationships would set individuals, communities, and nations free from the bondage and consequences of lying, hypocrisy, and deceit). But he was categorically asserting that it is possible for an individual to know *the truth*, as a divine absolute which Jesus himself had received from God his Father. As a result, that individual would be delivered from all the consequences of experienced bondage.

But, like jesting Pilate, it may be asked: "What is truth?" Archbishop William Temple gives this working definition:

"Truth is the objective apprehension of things as they are, in contrast to an apprehension or vision distorted by selfish desires and special interests."[7]

A restatement of the meaning of freedom, therefore, as Jesus taught it, would be: "*Freedom* is knowing the general and particular *truth* revealed by God the Father regarding his purpose in creation, and in perceiving and practicing that revealed truth."

In Archbishop Temple's words again, this would read: "The way to spiritual freedom...is always by surrender to the object—to the real facts in the life of science, to the goal or cause in practical conduct, to God as he reveals himself in worship."

At Pharmakon we taught that, to remain free from drugs, an individual has to become God-centered instead of self-centered, God-controlled instead of self-directed. For it is self-interest which is the bondage of the addict. He or she is not just in bondage to a chemical, as has been demonstrated by detoxification from its effects. The true bondage is the addiction to a life-style of impotence—even at the price of its accompanying self-loathing. It is not just the drug-free life which is empty; it is the inner self. It is not just the drug-free life which is without meaning; it is the inner self which is devoid of values.

A person has to have a belief if he or she is to have values—a belief that is more than a mere mental assent to a set of propositions. A value may be defined as: a belief freely chosen from among alternatives after careful consideration of the consequences of each alternative; a belief that is prized, so that the person is happy with the choice; a belief that is important enough that the person will publicly affirm the choice; a belief that is acted on repeatedly, over a period of time, and incorporated into a person's behavior.

To provide patients with the opportunity to find such a belief system, the Pharmakon Treatment emphasized three groups of values.

Creative values were inculcated by achieving specific tasks, starting with meditation and other exercises to provide a framework within which to experience a wider and deeper spiritual appreciation of life. Physical and emotional reeducation by means of various techniques for living were used to teach self-discipline as a start.

Experiential values were discovered by putting into practice fundamental principles learned at study or interaction groups during discussions of practical religion and philosophy, about what is right, good, true, beautiful, pure, just, etc. Involvement in a community where the lessons learned could be tested and proved was found to be essential.

Personal values included the correcting of "personality disorders" by spiritual means. Caring counsellors provided the individual with a sense of security, self-reliance, and self-confidence. The goal was to help the individual grasp the possibility of being a significant person with a meaningful role to play in the family and community. That sense of meaning was acquired by each individual in a framework of loving and being loved in a unique, specific, and personal way. The individuals who had come that far were encouraged to communicate their new sense of meaning to at least one other person so that he or she could share that uniqueness.

A family model

What this meant for us as a family was that my relations with my husband, and ours with our children, were under constant daily scrutiny by every addict. We ate, lived, worked with them on the principle that patients were to be treated as we treated each other. We did not ask them to do what we were not doing ourselves. If the results were good for us and our children, and the addicts liked what they saw, then it was likely to be good for them. That was what "loving your neighbor as yourselves" meant to us. We loved each other's company, and we were glad to share what we had as a family and as professionals with some experience of the addicts' problems; but that was because our lives were founded on spiritual values acquired in difficult experiences in several countries and cultures.

The aim of the doctor at all times must be to bring out the greatest potential of the patient, to realize his or her latent values. Goethe said: "If we take people as they are, we make them worse. If we treat them as if they were what they ought to be, we help them to become what they are capable of becoming." In this context, Dr. Frankl said: "To experience one human being as unique means to love him." And Dostoyevski summed it all up when he said: "To love a person means to see him as God intended him to be."

12 INDEPENDENT SUMMARY OF NET: CLINICAL RESEARCH

The one-year clinical trial funded by The Rank Foundation took place in 1980, January to December, at a medically-approved, nonprofit clinic, Broadhurst Manor in Sussex, England. The staff was qualified in all respects, except for the deliberate omission of psychiatric personnel, although some of the nursing staff had psychiatric training. The counselors were chosen on the basis of holding and practicing spiritual values in appropriate life situations, and were addressed regularly by my husband out of his own experience of spiritual values analyzed and practiced in over forty years in different countries with a variety of religions, customs, and ideologies.

There was no pre-selection process for admission for treatment, except for the usual initial medical consultations to establish that the patient had no psychosis or other condition impossible to treat at the Clinic.

Having a single unit for detoxification and rehabilitation dramatically increased the benefits of NET, as incoming patients saw others, whom they knew from their own experience should have been suffering, without the usual distress. It quickly became apparent that a whole new national and international approach to the treatment of addictions was going to be necessary because of the rapid detoxification and the subsequent—even concomitant—psychological benefit.

Attempts to set up controlled studies
I had tried several times to find funding for a double-blind study of NET, or a control group, to satisfy the usual medical and scientific requirements for any new form of treatment. Although I was not convinced of the usefulness of the double-blind process in this field, I made application to several funding bodies for funds to conduct a double-blind trial of NET. Those attempts included two applications, in 1975 and 1977, to the National Institute on Drug Abuse of the National Institutes of Health in Bethesda, Maryland. All were refused, and one of the stated reasons for refusal was that I had had no previous experience of research. Yet I knew of *no* experienced researcher who had a knowledge of NET! The fact is that very few controlled studies have been done to establish the efficacy of *any* treatment in the drug abuse field. Griffith Edwards, a well-known British psychiatrist in that field (who had appeared in the first BBC film about NET as an independent commentator in 1975), made a proposal for such studies:

"To date in this country, only one major controlled trial has been mounted on an aspect of drug treatment (Mitcheson and Hartnoll, 1978[1]). The most feasible and promising approach might indeed be to mount a series of relatively small scale studies which sequentially assess the effectiveness of particular elements within the total treatment package, either by means of controlled comparison groups or with patients used as their own controls."[2]

Other experts in the substance abuse treatment field have defended their own or others' failure to do such trials. In a detailed analysis of the U.S. government-supported Drug Abuse Reporting Program (DARP), analyzing 1,496 addicts participating in the research, D. D. Simpson commented:

"Although critics of field research to evaluate treatment outcomes suggest that the use of experimental procedures and randomized control groups is the ideal approach to a scientific determination that a treatment effect does or does not exist, this has not been proved feasible or an acceptable methodological alternative in most research on the effectiveness of drug-abuse treatment."[3]

In my own search of the literature I had found only one controlled study, and its was *not* a double-blind trial. That study used active or simulated cerebral electrotherapy (CET, which I have described elsewhere; it has a different electronic form and electrode placement from NET) or methadone detoxification, on twenty-eight methadone addicts. It was reported that ten of the thirteen patients receiving active CET were drug-free by the end of eight to ten days, and that all thirteen experienced a marked reduction of their symptoms. The control group did not show significant changes.[4] A preliminary double-blind study of human beta-endorphin administered intravenously to two addicts undergoing withdrawal from methadone indicated a reversal of symptoms after the injection and a feeling of normality.[5]

The clinical trial I designed for the Pharmakon Clinic, on the basis of my own experience, was actually along the lines which, three years later, Griffith Edwards proposed as ideal.

When the trial ended in December 1980, we were unable to persuade the British government to integrate the Clinic or treatment process within the British system—although in private they were highly complimentary. I decided that my next priority was to produce a statistical analysis of the year's clinical trial, and to begin follow-up research of patients I had treated in the previous seven years in England. (See Appendix XVII, p. 175.) Also, George, my husband, had been devising a new and more practical national and international approach to the addiction problem.

Our move to the United States
One of the biggest obstacles I had found to further development of NET was the negative attitude of people towards any treatment for addictions. From the government (which was having a difficult time finding money for reputable hospitals, and other important medical institutions), to charities (which felt that diseases such as cancer, or organizations for the physically or mentally handicapped should come first), to individuals (who said that addicts deserved to suffer for their self-imposed condition), it was obvious that fund-raising on the scale necessary for research, development, and treatment was not going to be forthcoming in Britain.

Once again an individual with an interest in my work, this time an American, enabled me to take the next step. Gordon H. Crowther was a friend of many years whom my husband had known professionally as a man with worldwide financial and business interests. Now a retired financial adviser, company chairman, inventor, and engineer, he had offered to help us whenever the clinical trial ended.

We went to California in the spring of 1981 where for patent and other reasons I decided that I would have to design another model of stimulator. For the next few months I worked with Walter Underhill, an electronics engineer, to devise a stimulator which would incorporate a number of new features developed from my recent clinical and laboratory experience. In addition to his electronics expertise Walter was able, intuitively and skillfully, to comprehend and solve the problems of turning my increasingly complex theories regarding bioelectric stimulation into technological realities. The new model would be based on my ten years experience of "fine-tuning" the stimulator to adapt to the daily, often hourly, changes in response to NET. The complexity of the problem can be judged by the multiplicity of the withdrawal symptoms of each different group of psychoactive drugs (see Appendix XVIII, p. 176.)

I completed the design of my new Model V NeuroElectric Stimulator in 1982. This model is not only much more advanced electronically than my previous models, but it also eliminates the principal hindrance to the rapid spread of NET—the necessity for in-depth training of medical personnel. Because it is fully programmed and automated, medical staff—or paramedics, under medical supervision—are now able to use NET effectively, after a careful study of the instruction booklet.

Overall medical supervision is still required because necessary precautions must be taken in the case of patients with heart disease, for example; or in taking patients off drugs which have the potential for causing convulsions in the withdrawal period. There is clinical evidence that NET markedly reduces the incidence of withdrawal convulsions, but my aim in research is to be able to eliminate these completely.

By the end of 1982 I had found funds to complete the statistical analysis and had submitted the findings to medical and scientific journals (Appendix XIX, p.179, describes a few of the most significant analyses). Then I was asked to write this book.

Gordon Crowther offered to set up an organization to incorporate the manufacture and distribution of NET stimulators worldwide, along with an associated research facility that would allow further development of NET as a possible means of treating conditions other than addictions. The groundwork for that multinational organization has been laid, and we are anticipating the setting up of clinics in many countries to use the Pharmakon Treatment psycho-spiritual methods which we had already found so effective.

Meanwhile, *Omni* a science magazine had heard of my work and after a ten-month investigation, in which the *Omni* associate editor Kathleen McAuliffe indefatigably and meticulously interrogated patients, colleagues, interested and skeptical doctors and scientists, they published a major article in the January 1983 issue. Because it gives an independent and admirable survey of NET based on exhaustive investigation I have asked Kathleen McAuliffe and the editors of *Omni* magazine for permission to reprint the entire article, plus an interview with Pete Townshend that accompanied it.

"Brain Tuner," by Kathleen McAuliffe

"It looks like a Walkman," explains Pete Townshend, the lead guitarist of and chief songwriter for The Who, the British rock band. "You clip this transistor-size unit onto your belt, and there's two wires leading from it that you attach behind your ears. Then it's a question of tuning in to the right frequency."

The thirty-eight-year-old rock star is not describing the latest advance in recording technology, but a novel treatment for drug addiction—a treatment that may work by striking a melodic chord in the brain. The Walkman look-alike transmits a tiny electrical signal that appears to harmonize with natural brain rhythms and, in the process, reduce craving and anxiety. Or at least it worked for Townshend. The little black box, he says, saved him from a nearly suicidal two-year alcoholic binge that eventually drove him to heavy tranquilizers and virtually any other drug he could get his hands on. "The treatment works not only for boozers," Townshend emphasizes. "It's helped people give up cigarettes, heroin, barbiturates, speed, cocaine, marijuana—you name it. There is a different frequency that works best for each kind of addiction."

Dr. Margaret Patterson, a Scottish surgeon currently residing in southern California, is the owner and inventor of this magical device. Her black box sounds suspiciously like quackery. Just twiddle a few knobs and—presto—you can be cured of every imaginable vice. But the magic is real to people in the rock 'n' roll industry, who call her a miracle worker. Apparently Townshend is not the only celebrity who has benefited from her unusual remedy. She is credited with having reformed more than a dozen top recording stars, including ex-heroin addicts Eric Clapton and the seemingly indestructable Keith Richards, of the Rolling Stones, whose reckless abuse of drugs became as legendary as his music. (For Townshend's personal account of combating drug addiction with Patterson's black box, see end of article).

Happily, Patterson does not fit the image of either a charlatan or a cult figure. She is in her fifties, slender of frame, with a kindly face that radiates compassion. Her pale blue eyes are set off by a magnificent mane of auburn hair, which is swept up into a graceful, oversized bun. "I hesitate to use the word *cure*," she says in a soft, lilting burr. "I prefer to call it a method of rapid detoxification. The electricity quickly cleanses the addict's system of drugs, restoring the body to normal within ten days. Most patients report that their craving also subsides in the process."

Patterson's electrical stimulator is currently pending clinical approval by the Food and Drug Administration (FDA) in the United States, where she has lived since 1981. Over the last decade in Britain, however, almost 300 addicts have received NeuroElectric Therapy (NET), the technical name for her treatment. Patterson claims that all but four were left drug-free at the end of the detoxification process—a remarkable 98 percent success rate. "NET should not be confused with ECT—electroconvulsive therapy for mental patients," she cautions. "NET is far milder, involving currents at least twenty times weaker. Patients feel only a slight tingling sensation behind their ears where the electrodes are taped on." Yet this "mild" therapy, she insists, will subdue the violent physiological reactions that can make "going cold turkey" intolerable for even the most strong-willed person. Though normally soft-spoken, Patterson asserts unequivocally, "I can take anyone off a drug of abuse, no matter how severe his or her addiction, with only minimal discomfort."

Of course, not all those who complete the detoxification program remain abstinent. Patterson emphasizes that NET is most effective when backed up by counseling, remedial training, and supportive home environment. For many individuals, however, the treatment does appear to have long-lasting effects. If we are to believe the recidivism figures she cites, they are many times lower than the national average for every class of addictive drug.

A glance at Patterson's credentials provides reassurance that she is both serious and highly capable. At twenty-one, she was the youngest woman to qualify as a doctor at Scotland's Aberdeen University. Only four years later she obtained her fellowship at the Royal College of Surgeons, at Edinburgh University—an elite circle that few penetrate before their thirties. And just before her fortieth birthday she was presented one of her native land's highest honors by the Queen—an M.B.E., or Member of the British Empire—for her outstanding medical work in India.

Colleagues and patients describe the tiny Scottish surgeon as warm, confident, and virtually unflappable. "You can't con her," says one patient who had spent years cheating and lying to get bigger drug prescriptions. "And if you try to put one over on her, she won't turn her back on you like other doctors."

"She's the sort of mother you always dreamed of having," says a female addict. Still another views her as a saintly figure "with the selfless devotion of someone like Mother Theresa."

Patterson's close rapport with her patients has made some professionals question whether her dazzling record in drug rehabilitation is really attributable to the powers of electricity. "It's her personality" is the chief disclaimer psychiatrists have attached to her work. "She doesn't control for psychological factors such as people's expectations," says Dr. Richard B. Resnick, an associate professor at New York Medical College, who is recognized as an innovator in the treatment of heroin addiction. "For example, what happens if you fasten electrodes to patients' heads but don't turn on the electricity? You just talk to them and feed them chicken soup. Will they do better, the same, or worse than the group that got current?"

Such skepticism is less common in England, where Patterson's clinical practice was based until recently. There, a number of doctors have already begun to obtain the same beneficial effects with her electrical stimulator model.

Dr. Margaret Cameron, a psychiatrist with the National Health Service, in Somerset, England, reports that NET gives "very, very good results—better than any other treatment I've encountered." Since May 1981, Dr. Cameron has treated forty alcoholics, two methadone addicts, four heroin addicts, and a few individuals with mixed addictions involving cocaine and barbiturates. In follow-up interviews conducted six months to a year later, sixty percent of the alcoholics were still off alcoholic beverages and none of the other patients had relapsed. A private practitioner based in New Jersey, Dr. Joseph Winston, shares Cameron's enthusiasm for NET. "As a benign, effective technique for withdrawing people from drugs, it is virtually unmatched."

If NET has met with resistance, it is because its mode of action strains the explanatory powers of modern science. Until recently orthodox medicine refused to recognize that infinitesimal electrical currents may influence the behavior or function of living organisms. Currents less than 100 millivolts—or below the threshold for triggering a nerve impulse—were assumed to have no effect on biological processes. This dogmatic view had to be reassessed when accounts of such unsettling phenomena began appearing with increasing frequency in technical journals over the last decade. NET is, in fact, only one branch of a young, controversial discipline that is still struggling to achieve respectability, the science of electrical medicine.

In the early Seventies scientists began introducing very small currents via electrodes to different parts of the body—with dramatic results. A rat amputee was induced to regrow a forelimb down to midjoint, according to one exciting—though sometimes contested—report. In human applications, the FDA has approved the use of such currents for stitching together bone fractures. Recent experimental trials also indicate that trickling flows of electricity promote the healing of chronic bed-sores, burns, and even peripheral-nerve injuries. The external currents, it is theorized, stimulate rapid healing by augmenting the body's internal currents.

"By contrast, weak currents applied to the brain affect different physiological processes," says Dr. Robert O. Becker, a pioneer of electrical medicine who recently retired from Veterans Administration Hospital, in Syracuse, New York. "But I believe Dr. Patterson is producing profound alterations of the central nervous system. The psychological set that makes a person become an addict seems to disappear."

Researchers are now starting to elucidate NET's scientific rationale, winning over new converts from the more conservative ranks of the medical profession. In the process, Patterson's black box is helping to unlock the mysterious inner workings of that other black box: the human brain. The stimulus goes in and the response comes out, but seldom are we afforded a glimpse of what happens in between. By probing NET's effects on experimental animals, investigators are shedding light on the underlying mechanisms that control everything from addictive behavior to our most basic drives and emotions. As Dr. Becker surmised, the stimulator does indeed cause "profound alterations of the nervous system." Underlying consciousness is an intricate orchestral arrangement of trillions of brain cells, firing in concert. Like different instruments in a symphony, subpopulations of neurones are now believed to produce frequencies within a specific range. Frequency, so to speak, is the music of the hemispheres.

Like penicillin and X-rays, NET was born of scientific serendipity. It began with an accidental discovery in the fall of 1972. At that time Patterson was head of surgery at Hong Kong's Tung Wah Hospital, a large charity institution with a poor clientele. A neurosurgeon colleague, Dr. H. L. Wen, had just returned from the People's Republic of China, where he had learned the techniques of electroacupuncture. Primarily interested in its usefulness in the suppression of pain, he began testing it on patients with a variety of ills. Dr. Wen, however, did not know that almost 15 percent of his patients were addicted to heroin or opium of extremely high purity. At that time their drugs were easily affordable at a daily cost of less than a pack of cigarettes.

"One day," Patterson recalls, "an addict approached Dr. Wen, announcing that the electroacupuncture had stopped his withdrawal symptoms. 'I felt as if I'd just had a shot of heroin,' he said. Wen initially thought nothing of it, but a few hours later another addict reported a similar experience, equating the electroacupuncture with a certain dosage of opium."

Further inquiries revealed that a few alcoholics and cigarette smokers in Wen's experimental group had also been freed from their craving. To the eye, however, the electroacupuncture produced the most dramatic response in the narcotics addicts deprived of their drugs. The characteristic runny nose, stomach cramps, aching joints, and feeling of anxiety usually disappeared after ten to fifteen minutes stimulation by needles inserted inside the hollow of the external ear, at the acupuncturist's lung point. At first these good effects lasted only a few hours. But with repeated treatments, patients remained symptom-free for periods of longer duration.

The results of Wen's first study with forty opiate addicts were published in the *Asian Journal of Medicine* the following spring. Of this group, thirty-nine were drug-free by the time they left the hospital, roughly two weeks after starting treatment. When Patterson returned to England in July 1973, however, she found that addicts were far less enthusiastic about the procedure. The Chinese loved acupuncture; the British hated it. "As bizarre as it may sound," Patterson explains, "Westerners—even those who mainlined drugs—often had an aversion to needles."

There was another reason not to use the needles. Patterson had suspected from the outset that acupuncture was essentially an electrical phenomenon. Even the traditional explanation hinted that this might be so. The ancient practice revolves around the notion that all living things possess vital energy, called *chi*, which circulates through the body by way of a network of channels, or "meridians." Sickness was seen to be the result of disharmony, manifested by an obstruction in the flow of *chi*, which the needling was thought to remedy.

Was *chi* the ancients' concept for what modern man now recognizes as the internal currents that course through the body? Could it be that the Chinese, more than 2,500 years before the discovery of electricity, had intuitively sought to alter this life force in an attempt to alleviate pain and to cure disease? Perhaps, Patterson reasoned, the twirling of needles generates a tiny electrical voltage. Viewed in this light, the more recent practice of electroacupuncture was simply a more intense form of the original twirling technique. If so, the electrical signal would be of crucial significance in the treatment of addictions.

Years of clinical trial and error eventually confirmed her hunch. First Patterson replaced the needles with electrodes. The she went on to compare direct current with alternating current, while varying the voltage, shape, and other aspects of the electrical signal. Next she altered the electrode placement, finding a position just behind the ear over the mastoid bone to be more effective than the lung point. But, of all the variables explored, electrical frequency quickly emerged as the single most important element for success. Those addicted to narcotics and sedatives preferred frequencies within the 75 hertz to 300 hertz range, barbiturate addicts responded to lower frequencies, and still other addicts, especially those dependent on cocaine and amphetamines, benefited most from frequencies as high as 2,000 hertz. "Musicians," she fondly recalls, "really helped to strengthen my guesswork during those early days. They invariably found the correct therapeutic setting right away. It was as if their brains were more attuned to frequency."

A further refinement of the therapy was prompted by still another fortuitous discovery: A heavy abuser fell asleep with the stimulator on and awoke 30 hours later, well-rested and eager to take Patterson children ice-skating. From that moment onward, Patterson advocated continuous current application in the initial phases of treatment. She began the search for more comfortable electrodes that could be worn during sleep and for smaller electrical simulators that could be clipped onto belts, permitting mobility during the day.

By 1976 Patterson had transformed electroacupuncture into an exciting new experimental treatment mode that she christened NeuroElectric Therapy. In her first clinical study, which was reported that year in the U. N. *Bulletin on Narcotics*, opiate addicts given NET as in-patients were all found to be drug-free an average of ten months after completing treatment. In contrast, opiate addicts who received NET only during the day as out-patients did not fare as well: 47 percent were drug-free at the time of the follow-up.

Because this preliminary investigation was limited to 23 patients, her results could not be extrapolated to a larger cross section of addicts. To provide better information about the long-term effects of NET, and also to assess its value in the treatment of other kinds of addictions, Patterson was recently awarded a research grant by the British Medical Association.

Last fall, at a Washington, D.C., symposium sponsored by the American Holistic Medical Association, Patterson presented the findings from this follow-up evaluation, which tracked the progress of patients treated between 1973 and 1980. Data were obtained from confidential questionnaires and, when possible, from personal interviews. Fifty percent responded to the survey, and these respondents included sixty-six drug addicts (mostly mainline heroin or methadone users and mixed-addiction cases), nine cigarette smokers, and eighteen alcoholics. At the time of the follow-up, total abstinence was said to be achieved by 80 percent of the drug addicts, 44 percent of the cigarette smokers, and 78 percent of the alcoholics who stated abstinence to be their goal. An additional seven alcoholics whose goal on admission was 'controlled drinking' all reported success. (As Patterson herself cautions, however, these figures probably represent too favorable an outcome since patients who relapsed, especially alcoholics, may have been less likely to reply to the survey.) Of those who were successfully weaned from their dependence, 68 percent said they never or only rarely experienced craving, 15 percent said they occasionally felt craving, and another 17 percent said they frequently felt craving.

Interestingly, none of the drug addicts at the time of reporting had substituted alcohol for their earlier addiction—a finding that contrasts sharply with the figures cited in other studies. In one national survey, for example, 60 percent of addicts who had given up narcotics became heavy drinkers or alcoholics. Equally noteworthy was the equally low dropout rate of all addicts enrolled in the program: only 1.6 percent did not complete the detoxification.

All things considered, the success of Patterson's patients is probably the most remarkable from the standpoint of the brief duration of the therapy, which, including counseling, rarely extends beyond 30 days. According to a large study of drug abusers admitted to a variety of government-sponsored programs, addicts treated less than three months did not fare any better than those in a no-treatment comparison group. So NET seems to achieve in a few weeks what few, if any, orthodox treatments can accomplish after months or years.

Not everyone, however, is convinced by the report's conclusions. A look at the history of drug reform in the United States shows that their cynicism is not ill-founded. Consider the government's efforts to curb narcotics use. The first U. S. Public Health Service hospital for heroin addicts opened in Lexington, Kentucky, where 18,000 patients were admitted between 1935 and 1952. All except some 7 percent of the alumni promptly relapsed after dismissal from the institution—a dreary record that other institutions scarcely improved upon in subsequent decades.

By the 1960s heroin addiction had spread like cancer through inner-city ghettos. To control the expanding epidemic, health professionals turned to methadone, a synthetic opiate that is legally prescribed. Today thousands of clinics throughout the nation dispense methadone to certified addicts, and those maintained in these programs show higher rates of employment and fewer criminal offenses than before they began treatment. But methadone, alas, is even more addictive than heroin. As one medical authority points out, "The tragedy of methadone is that we cannot get people off methadone."

For narcotics addicts who aspire to a drug-free existence, society offers two main alternatives: the highly structured and insulated environments of such residential homes as Daytop Village, Phoenix House and Odyssey House or out-patient clinics, which provide daily counseling services. As many as 30 to 40 percent of the people who enroll in these community-based programs remain abstinent a year after leaving treatment. But to enter most of these programs, one must first detoxify in a hospital. And here's the hitch: 64 percent don't make it past the acute withdrawal phase to qualify for further treatment.

"It is still not understood why simple detoxification is so ineffective, but the facts are clear and inescapable," says Dr. Avram Goldstein, professor of pharmacology at Stanford University. "As I see it, the reason for the dismal failure...is that the newly detoxified addict, still driven by discomfort, physiologic imbalance, and intense craving, cannot focus attention on the necessary first steps toward rehabilitation, but soon succumbs and starts using heroin."

Jean Cocteau, the French writer, who resumed smoking after medicine had "purged" him of the habit, put it another way: "Now that I am cured, I feel empty, poor, heartbroken and ill."

In sharp contrast, NET patients are said to emerge from treatment feeling healthy, energetic, even cheerful. Dr. Joseph Winston, the American physician who collaborated with Patterson in the treatment of Keith Richards, recalls that the musician "came to us terribly ill. He was literally *green*. But he slept eighteen hours the first day, and ten days later he was playing tennis, and the group said he had not looked so good in years."

If Patterson's findings seem at total variance with the bulk of the clinical literature, the firsthand accounts of NET patients may help explain why.

Stuart Harris started shooting heroin as a sixteen-year-old cadet in the Royal Navy. By the time he underwent NET in the spring of 1981, he had been addicted to heroin fifteen years, and for eleven of those years he had also injected methadone intravenously. "I had the sweats very badly," he says of his experience on NET. "You're emitting all this bad grunge from your body, and you feel you're speeding (on amphetamines). But there's no withdrawal at all. That much I'll say for it. I mean when they told me about it, I just took it with a pinch of salt—another treatment they've fobbed off on the poor junkies. But, believe me, if I was getting any pain as I used to have with withdrawals, I wouldn't have stayed there, 'cause I was a voluntary patient. When I discharged myself from hospital, I didn't go searching for drugs as I would normally have done in the past, say, after methadone reduction or narcosis (that's when they sedate you up to your eyeballs in sleeping pills). After completing all the other methods, I felt so uptight all the time. The first thing I wanted to do was have a massive great fix. But, after NET, all you really want to do is sleep. Everything is so easygoing. I can't say that it (heroin) doesn't drift into my mind. Like the other day, I fancied a fix. But it passed over in a few minutes. Before, if I'd felt the slightest urge for a fix, off I'd go to London. Something has changed. You feel calmer. You can accept the ups and downs."

A man in his thirties, who requested anonymity, had injected heroin for eight years, combining this dose with prescribed methadone during the last five years of the period. He received NET in 1974. "The treatment was rough," he said. "I felt as if I had a mild case of the flu, combined with short periods of feeling spaced out—even a bit euphoric. My anxiety and craving subsided right from the beginning, but a few weeks later my craving for heroin went back up again. I wanted to go out again and score. And, as a matter of fact, I did. But, it was different. It wasn't satisfying. It didn't make me feel that great. I know this treatment changed my head, because I never thought about heroin again after that. You see, I had gotten off heroin for as much as a month, even two months, at a stretch. But the whole of that time I would be thinking of heroin and nothing else."

A twenty-eight-year-old man, who also requested anonymity, combined a high level of alcohol and marijuana consumption with a cocaine habit of two to six grams each week for more than seven years. (The cocaine alone usually cost him more than $1,000 a month.) He agreed to speak to *Omni* immediately after completing NET treatment in the summer of 1982. "Until this therapy," he says, "I couldn't go three days without feeling an enormous craving for drugs. Cocaine and, to a lesser degree, alcohol would always be on my mind. But from the moment the electrodes were put on my head, my craving immediately diminished. When I had passed the three-day mark, I felt no craving at all, and I still don't. Drugs never enter my mind. Now that I remember what it's like to feel good—to be clearheaded after all these years—I'm certain that I won't go back on drugs."

Rachel Waite, a heavy smoker for five years, was treated for her cigarette addiction in June 1981. "For the first three days on NET," she recalls, "I still had the urge to smoke, and I probably would have lit up had a cigarette been handy. However, by the end of the treatment I definitely did not want one. When I took an experimental puff, it was a different sensation altogether. It tasted foul, and there was no hit whatsoever. It was as if I was drawing on hot air."

Surprisingly, many patients who go on to build drug-free lives do not receive any formal counseling beyond that provided during the brief detoxification program. Yet NET, by itself, cannot remove the root causes of addiction, nor can it replace years of maladaption with healthy skills for coping with life's stresses and disappointments. Why then do so many patients experience such a metamorphosis?

The treatment, Patterson believes, simply sets the stage for further growth. "Because they feel so good," she says, "they are better able to face the sort of problems that drove them to addiction in the first place. You see, most people who come off drugs without NET enter a phase of prolonged dysphoria. They suffer from fearful depression and pessimism. They can't eat. They can't sleep. They have no energy. This can last for six months in the case of heroin, and even longer in the case of methadone and barbiturate addiction. But NET restores physiological normality within ten days, which enormously reduces the amount of time needed for readjustment."

If anything, Patterson thinks that euphoria—not dysphoria—is to blame when rehabilitation fails. The newly detoxified addict is optimistic to the point of being overconfident. "In their elated state," Patterson says, "they think it will be easy to stay off drugs and then end up stumbling, because they don't make enough of an effort to change their ways."

As if obeying Newtonian mechanics, the black box appears to counter one mood shift with an equal swing in the opposite direction, until the emotional pendulum finally comes to rest. Is the black box, in reality, an electronic substitute for a chemical high? How can a physical treatment cause such a swing towards euphoria?

As fate would have it, a scientist who had taught Patterson years earlier, Dr. Hans Kosterlitz, would once again serve as her mentor by illuminating the mainspring of euphoria in the brain. While working with Dr. John Hughes at the University of Aberdeen in 1975, Dr. Kosterlitz identified an endorphin, a natural brain chemical, with a molecular structure very similar to the opiates. For this outstanding discovery, the investigators later received the prestigious Lasker Award, revered as America's equivalent of the Nobel Prize in medicine. Almost overnight their finding triggered an explosion in the understanding of the biochemical basis of behavior, opening a new vista on the controlling factors behind addiction. Opium, heroin, morphine, and other related drugs owe their potency to what Avram Goldstein calls "one of nature's most bizarre coincidences"—their uncanny resemblance to the endorphins.

Over the succeeding years researchers uncovered evidence of myriad other brain hormones that mimic psychoactive drugs, from Valium and angel dust to hallucinogens. Almost every mind-altering substance, it is now assumed, has an analogue in the brain. And the precise mixture of neurojuices in this biochemical cocktail can mean the difference between tripping, speeding, crashing or seeing the world through sober eyes.

These insights immediately suggested how the addict becomes trapped in a nightmarish cycle of dependency. In the initial phases of narcotic use, for example, the individual is assumed to have normal levels of endorphins in the brain. Injecting heroin causes a sudden and drastic elevation of opiates, which is subjectively interpreted as ecstasy. If through repeated use the brain is regularly flooded with opiates, it redresses the imbalance by cutting back on the production of its internal supply. Hence, the well-known condition of tolerance develops. The addict steps up his dosage, and the brain further compensates by calling a massive shutdown of production. Eventually, according to the theory, the addict is shooting up solely for the purpose of "feeling normal." Should the drug supply be cut off at this stage, the opiate shortage cannot be instantly remedied. Drought ensues, unleashing withdrawal symptoms.

If an exogenous drug depletes the brain of its natural counterpart, it seemed logical that NET might quite literally juice up the system, rapidly replenishing the scarce neurochemical. Might certain frequencies of current catalyze the release of different brain hormones? Patterson wondered.

To find out, she conducted animal experiments in collaboration with biochemist Dr. Ifor Capel at the Marie Curie Cancer Memorial Foundation Research Department, in Surrey, England. Simply by monitoring the blood of NET-treated rats, the investigators discovered low-frequency currents can indeed cause as much as a three-fold elevation of endorphin levels.

In another experiment the researchers examined NET's effects on rats rendered unconscious by massive doses of barbiturates. Once asleep, all the animals had electrodes clipped on to their ears, but only half the group actually received electrical current. The result: At one particular frequency—ten hertz—the experimental group rapidly regained consciousness, sleeping on average 40 percent less than the rats that received no electricity.

Why is the detoxification process hastened? One clue surfaced when the rats' brain tissue was analyzed. It was learned that the ten-hertz signal speeds up the production and turnover rate of serotonin (a neurotransmitter that acts as a stimulant to the central nervous system).

Similar experiments have now been repeated on rats made unconscious by injecting them with alcohol or ketamine (a cousin of angel dust). In almost every instance the frequencies that reduced sleeping time had earlier been proved therapeutic in the detoxification of human addicts. "Virtually every single parameter of current that I had stumbled upon during my clinical work was corroborated by the rat studies," Patterson declares, with barely concealed excitement.

How a weak electrical current can open the floodgates of the mind is still a matter of conjecture, but the implications are obvious. Like a citizen's-band transmitter that infiltrates television frequencies, the black box must broadcast through brain frequency channels. And just as a TV receiver can pick up CB transmissions from a passing truck, the brain undoubtedly responds to the foreign-generated signal as if it originated from within its own communication network.

"As far as we can tell," says Dr. Capel, a rugged Welshman with a melodic voice," each brain center generates impulses at a specific frequency based on the predominant neurotransmitters it secretes. In other words, the brain's internal communications system—its language—if you like—is based on frequency."

Unfortunately, neuroscientists are not yet fluent in this new tongue. "NET is still a very blunt tool," Capel acknowledges. "Presumably, when we send in waves of energy at, say, ten hertz, certain cells in the lower brain stem will respond, because they normally fire at that frequency range. As a result, particular mood-altering chemicals associated with that region will be released. That's what we *hope* is happening. In reality, however, much of the signal may be lost before it actually reaches the target cells. We just don't know. But if we can fine-tune the signal, I am confident our results will steadily improve."

At her small two-bedroom home in Corona del Mar Patterson has begun testing a new, improved model of the stimulator. Her goal—and the major impetus behind her decision to come to the United States—is to obtain funding for the establishment of a center where human and animal research can proceed in tandem. Until FDA clearance is given, however, she cannot begin treating addicts on a routine basis.

Will NET open a new route to salvation for the millions of Americans who each year flock to Alcoholics Anonymous, Smoke Enders, and methadone maintenance clinics? Clearly the final verdict is contingent upon replication of controlled studies. But if a feeble electrical current can truly curb the mind's excesses—from uncontrollable lusts to extremes of mood—its impact is due to be far-reaching.

"Addicts may represent only a tiny fraction of the people who will eventually be helped by NET," Capel predicts. "In all likelihood it will find an enormous range of uses, especially in the area of pain control." In one preliminary trial, terminal patients suffering from chronic pain found NET just as effective as their daily dose of morphine. "By stimulating the brain's own pain-killer, we didn't have to administer drugs," Capel marvels.

Early data also indicate that NET may prove highly promising in the treatment of mental disorders. The frequencies that induce euphoria and reduce tension, according to Dr. Cameron, of Britain's National Health Service, "seem to work wonders for patients suffering from severe depression and acute anxiety." Though it is far too soon to draw any conclusions, she notes that "a few of the half-dozen chronic depressives we've treated have found themselves jobs after years of unemployment."

As for Patterson, she hopes eventually to broaden her practice to include behavioral addicts, from overeating and compulsive gambling to video-game fanaticism. Absurdity aside, these applications follow a certain logic. "Her ideas make perfect sense if one accepts the idea that behavioral addictions have a chemical basis," says Dr. William Regelson, at the Medical College of Virginia. "It is very likely, for example, that all activities vital to survival—from sex to physical exercise—are physiologically addictive. It is now thought that the phenomenon called jogger's high is actually endorphin-mediated. In all probability, eating also releases some kind of pleasurable molecule. After all, why do we crave food? Low blood-sugar levels don't explain why. The truth is that we feel abnormal when we haven't eaten in a while. Some chemical in our brain has become depleted. We become restless and agitated, and, after extreme deprivation, we suffer withdrawal symptoms commonly known as hunger pangs. The only way to relieve our discomfort is to get more food. It's a fix—plain and simple."

If basic drives are addictive, then drugs are an ingenious means of short-cutting the elaborate scheme nature devised to ensure that we maintain health and reproduce ourselves. Merely by popping a pill, we can top off our neurochemical reservoirs with no sweat expended. Instant orgasm without foreplay. A cheap thrill.

But can't the same be said of NET? "Is it not, after all, an electronic fix?" asks Regelson, who fears the black box may become addictive in its own right. Patterson has kept her eyes open to any signs that her patients are becoming physically dependent on the equipment. But she rules out the possibility that there will ever be a black market in the black boxes, because individual models can cost upward of $1,000—a hefty sum to cough up for purely recreational use. Besides, she has not encountered a single instance of electronic addiction in her ten years of practice. The explanation, she believes, "is that drugs—for the very reason that they are foreign—upset the brain's chemistry. NET, on the other hand, simply coaxes the brain to restore its own chemical balance. The body heals itself."

The intuitive feelings of her patients support this view. As reformed heroin addict Stuart Harris says, "At first I thought it would be fun to wire up the human race, so we could all go whizzing about. But after the initial buzz, you feel, well, normal. Frankly, all NET does is to help you face reality."

Patterson concurs: "All we can do is give people a chance. We can get them off whatever drug they're hooked to, but it's up to them to fill the void. They've got to find a constructive substitute for the drugs that have dominated their lives."[6]

In an accompanying interview in *Omni* magazine entitled "Pete Townshend On The Black Box," Pete Townshend gave his impressions of NET, both as used on himself and as he had seen it in the operative treatment of others in the past eight years. Pete had first seen NET when he visited Eric Clapton during his treatment, and was so impressed that over the next few years he and his rock group The Who raised many thousands of dollars to help me with my research.

The Who guitarist Pete Townshend traces his downward slide toward drugged oblivion to the troubled spring of 1980. Long months of touring had brought him to the brink of a marital rift. Gross financial mismanagement had left him $1 million in debt to English banks. And all the while he brooded incessantly about the future of The Who. "I started drinking about a bottle and a half of cognac a day, "Townshend recalls. "And to cut through the drunken stupor I was in, I got into this deadly alcohol-cocaine oscillation. Eventually I became such a physical wreck that I went to this doctor, who prescribed me sleeping pills and an anti-depressant called Ativan. These Ativans made me feel great, and soon I was taking eight to ten tablets a day, plus three sleeping pills every night. By Christmas, though, the Ativan stopped working, and so I turned to heroin. A month later it dawned on me that I was actually dying, that my macho 'I-can-do-anything' mentality would kill me. It was then I contacted Meg (Margaret Patterson).

"Even though I'd seen startling successes with her technique, I didn't know whether it would work for me. But by the second day I knew I was on the home straight. And on the third day I felt feelings of sexual desire returning, feelings of just wanting to go for walk. It was incredible! There was a sense of inner joy as I started to gain independence from drugs. A natural energy flow slowly returned to my body. I could feel the old me coming back, and the first emotion I felt was arrogance. I thought, 'This will be easy. A few more days on this machine, and then I'll shoot up to L.A. and go dancing.' That was my frame of mind. But the fourth day I got depressed. Initially I had been given low frequencies for heroin, but when I became depressed, I was given some high frequencies for my cocaine addiction. And at this high setting, I would sometimes have psychedelic experiences. The colors in the room would suddenly start to go wooo. Then I had another setback, followed by a day when I felt superhuman. It was just like being on heroin. But the next day I again felt like death warmed over. Some withdrawal symptoms even returned.

"Gradually, though, your mood levels off so that by the tenth day you feel fairly normal. In retrospect, I realize that the treatment is an education in itself. NET reeducates the brain to produce its own drugs, and in the process you learn something about your human potential. You come to realize that somewhere within you is the power to deal with crises, tensions and frustrations. So the treatment reaffirms one's faith in the self-healing process.

"Of course it seems incredibly crude to shoot a thousand-cycle pulse through the brain—and *voila!* Yet that's the beauty of it. There's something almost mystical about recovering by such a ridiculously simple technique. Somehow a simple little gadget has made me feel whole. And if I'm ever raped by a crazed pusher and become hooked all over again, I won't hesitate to call Meg and have my addiction handled in this straightforward, completely technical way."[7]

POSTSCRIPT

Despite the monumental scale of the drug problem, despite the lip-service paid by governments and medical groups to the seriousness of the problem, despite the fact that both of those groups admit that, to their knowledge, there is no promising cure for the treatment of addictions on the horizon, I have received from them only polite and professional expressions of interest—and no financial aid. The media—bless them!—despite their own vested interest in pursuing the bizarre and the sensational, have discharged their responsibility to the public with regard to my work with serious and balanced presentations since 1973. So the professional politicians in governments and medical establishments are without excuse in their reluctance—or even neglect—to pursue the *minimum* investigations.

As this is being written, the U. S. administration has been giving great publicity to a new policy to deal with "the drug problem." The President and Mrs. Reagan are both publicly identified with the five-fold program: (1) international cooperation; (2) drug law enforcement; (3) education and prevention; (4) detoxification and treatment; (5) research. The first two items have been highly publicized and funding has been sought to pursue them—and rightly so. But I know of no program, or funding, or publicity on a similar scale for the other three items—and that is where the primary problem lies.

Nor is the United States alone in this attitude. The British government has just announced a new commitment to dealing with the escalating drug and alcohol problems. The government's social services spokesman used words such as these: "...The Government recognizes the challenge...a major social problem with grave consequences that we cannot ignore... advisory council's report will be distributed to health authorities... arranging for a special conference of doctors early in the new year...to encourage new initiatives, $4 million to be made available to enable schemes to be brought forward in 1982-83...over-riding policy first to contain the drug problem, then to reduce it...treatment facilities to be developed..."[1]

The *Economist,* from which these excerpts were taken, is extremely skeptical about the British Government's commitment to its spokesman's statements. The *British Medical Journal* was also skeptical. In a lead article entitled "An Absence of Alcohol Policy" it questioned another government spokesman's attempts "to give the impression that the Government did have a strategy. In our opinion he failed." The article continued:

"The Central Policy Review Staff's report on alcohol policies (which the Government refused to publish in 1979 but which was published this year in Sweden by Professor Kettil Bruun, who also spoke at the conference) concluded that 'neither the existing machinery within Government, nor the bodies outside it, provide the means for coherent formulation of policies...' It recommended that an advisory council on alcohol policies should be established with associated internal coordinating arrangements. This recommendation, we suspect, is the one that particularly upset the Government and caused it to suppress the report. The Government does not want a coherent policy—it wants to have its cake and eat it. It wants the $5395-plus millions brought in through a tax on alcohol, and the 750,000 jobs supplied by the drink trade, and the $750 million brought in by the alcohol exports. It also wants to keep the good will of the powerful alcohol industry (Mr. J. B. Hanbury of the Brewers' Society told the conference that our three biggest breweries are all in the top fifty British companies), and of the advertising companies, which have an income of over $150 million a year from promoting the sale of alcohol.

"Of course, the Government wants to be seen to be doing something about alcohol misuse, and Mr. Finsberg told the conference of what we believe to be essentially 'symbolic' action to be agreed on by his department..."[2]

At the time of this writing the availability of NET stimulators, the groundwork for our own multinational organization has been completed. The NET stimulators will be available for any countries interested in doing something about their addiction problems (about twenty of which have been in touch with me over the past few years). Many are not just interested in the NET stimulators for detoxification of addictions, but also in the psycho-spiritual treatment program we have developed for rehabilitation—and transformation—of the addicted, and several books are in the process of publication to meet this demand.

So the "thousand-league journey" which began with the "one step" in Hong Kong in 1972 is nearing completion, and I would like to thank all those who made the journey possible and memorable. They are still helping and, like myself, experiencing the rewards promised to those who pursue a distant vision with faith and commitment. But many others will be needed to complete the task: the transformation of an uncaring, materialist society into one with compassionate spiritual vision and values.

Meanwhile, the nineteen countries who adumbrated the scale of the addiction problem in the West, in their Report of the Council of Europe (Strasbourg, 1970) in the following statement, also outlined their recommended solutions.

The Problem Stated

It is important to have in mind that this subject includes not only psychological and medical but also social, educational, cultural and political aspects. The increase in the dimensions of the problem can be looked upon as a symptom that there is something very wrong with society.

The problem is 'a problem neither of youth nor one of drugs, but a problem of a whole society and an entire life-style shared by young and old alike'...

Recommended Solutions to the Problem

In the light of the information received from the national health administrations and of the findings by the members of the team, it appears that the spread of drug dependence has reached epidemic proportions in the 19 countries surveyed.

This epidemic is still increasing and, in view of the lack of complete, accurate and up-to-date information, there is no possibility of forecasting its course, dimensions and duration.

Bearing in mind the importance of drug dependence in Europe and in view of the fact that:

(a) drug dependence is spreading alarmingly and rapidly amongst juveniles (in some European cities at least 25 percent of juvenile groups are at present involved) and that new patterns in drug dependence among juveniles are developing;

(b) drug dependence is increasing in whole populations, especially dependence on those drugs which are not yet under international narcotics control;

(c) there is a real danger of the formation of a whole sub-culture;

(d) there is a serious lack of information;

(e) a detailed program is needed if prevention and treatment are to be successful.

While considering that the actual facts of the problem are changing from month to month, the study group feels the necessity for carrying out further studies in the field and for taking immediate measures.

It therefore brings the following recommendations to the attention of the governments concerned.

Information
1. *It is recommended that, in each member country, data relating to different types of drug dependence and the personal status of the drug dependent should be collected on a local, national and European level, on the basis of a European standardized questionnaire. Such a questionnaire should be drawn up under the responsibility of the Council of Europe. A regular exchange of information collected on the basis of such a questionnaire should be organized and maintained on local, national and European levels. In every country an appropriate organ should be set up to collect and evaluate the information and to advise the government in so far as is necessary.*

Research
2. *With a view to prevention and treatment in each country concerned, experts in the field of drug dependence should be appointed to carry out prospective epidemiological studies and other research projects (i.e psychic and physical dependence, biochemistry and pharmacological aspects, personality of the drug dependent, group dynamics of adolescent drug users, new methods for education of the public and the professions concerned with this problem).*

Treatment
3. *Considering the lack of adequate treatment facilities for drug dependents, hospital beds should be made available as urgently as possible. In addition, new special institutions for treatment and after-care should be set up for rehabilitation. Particular attention should be paid to the training of specialized staff able to carry out the treatment.*

Prevention
4. *In each of the countries concerned, continuous prospective research should be undertaken to detect from the outset new trends in drug abuse, with a view to taking immediate and coordinated preventive measures.*
5. *Public opinion should be kept currently informed of the dangers of drug dependence. Private agencies should be established with governmental assistance to advise on and prepare material, designed for the informa-*

tion of the population. *Well-conceived educational programmes are essential for successful prevention through mass media, schools and clubs, in cooperation with juveniles, parents, teachers, psychologists, social workers, psychiatrists and ex-addicts. Supervised studies should check the efforts and the success of preventive endeavours.*

6. *Consultative centers should be available for juveniles who are anxious to obtain professional advice on and assistance in their efforts to free themselves from the danger of a tendency toward drug dependence, without fear of penal prosecution.*

7. *While the drug-abuser—whether a beginner or already dependent—is a medical problem, the drug trafficker is a legal one and severe punitive measures should be taken against anyone who derives profit from the craving of the dependent individual or seduces the uninitiated to become drug dependent.*

Co-ordination

8. *An appropriate center in one of the member States of the Council of Europe should be entrusted with:*

    (a) the collection and dissemination of information;

    (b) the co-ordination and national research at an international level and promotion of joint research;

    (c) new proposals for research, prevention and treatment programmes...

To the best of my knowledge, no serious attempt—if any—has been made by the nineteen countries who produced these recommendations, or others, to implement, investigate or propose a financial solution to a social evil "of epidemic proportions"—even although it often involves the families of the very legislators, statesmen and politicians who draw up the programs, or even themselves.

APPENDIX I

In his book, *The Puzzle of Pain,* discussing these and other findings, Dr. Ronald Melzack describes the inhibitory effect that the central tegmental tract had on input:

"The inhibitory influence may help to explain an exciting recent discovery. Reynolds (1969, 1970) has observed that electrical stimulation in the region of the central grey and central tegmental tract produces a marked analgesia in rats, so that they fail to respond to pinch, burn, even major abdominal surgery...More recently, Mayer, Akil and Liebeskind (1971) observed the same phenomenon, and found, moreover, that there is some somatotopic organization within the system, so that stimulation at a given site produces analgesia of only selected positions of the body, such as the lower half, or one quadrant. They found, furthermore, that the electrical stimulation of these areas appears 'pleasurable' to the animals—they actively seek it out by pressing a lever to stimulate themselves. These observations...have great theoretical significance since they suggest the presence of a system that exerts a tonic, widespread inhibitory influence on transmission through the somatosensory projection system..."[1]

APPENDIX II

The "gate theory" of pain control was that it had been demonstrated physiologically that all pain information travels to the spinal cord via small unmyelinated C fibers, and that stimulation of the larger myelinated A fibers was never painful. Further, activity in the large A fibers inhibited, at the first spinal synapse, immediate subsequent activity from the smallest fibers considered essential to pain conduction. Dr. Wall and Dr. Melzack suggested that this mechanism normally acted as a "gate" to balance pain and non-pain input.

APPENDIX III

In 1946, Dr. Grey Walter decided to try imposing new patterns of the existing brain rhythms through the senses. He began by flashing a light at regular intervals into the subject's eyes, and found that this flicker produced a new, strange pattern on the graphs. At certain frequencies the flicker also produced violent reactions in the subject, who was suddenly seized by what seemed to be an epileptic fit.

Grey Walter also noted the similarity of a natural epileptic seizure and one induced by electric shock therapy. He then turned his investigations to normal, resting brain waves of known epileptics, and found that their brain rhythms were grouped in certain frequencies. In order to keep the flicker and the brain synchronized, a feedback system in automatic control was adopted in the form of a trigger-circuit, the flash being fired by the brain rhythms themselves at any chosen time-relation with the rhythmic component of the spontaneous or evoked activity. With this instrument the effects of the flicker were found to be even more drastic than when the stimulus was fixed by an operator, in that in more than 50 percent of young normal adult subjects the first exposure to feedback flicker evoked transient paroxysmal discharges of the type seen so often in epileptics. He said: 'It was as if certain major chords constantly appeared against the trills and arpeggios of the normal activity."

He went on to report that the harmonic grouping suggested to him that all that was necessary to get the rhythms to synchronize in a tremendous explosion was an outside co-ordinator, a conductor who could bring the separate chords together in a simultaneous grand convulsion. A flicker in the alpha-rhythm range, between 8 and 12 cycles per second, acted in just this way on epileptics, provoking them into a seizure at any time. This technique had become a valuable clinical aid in the diagnosis of epilepsy.

In the 1920s a German psychiatrist, Hans Berger, had recorded the first human electro-encephalogram from platinum wires he had pushed into his son's scalp. Berger had surmised that the brain produced only one wave, but he soon discovered that electrodes placed on different parts of the scalp recorded different patterns, indicating various brain waves.

From these investigations there emerged the theory of four basic rhythmic patterns, which were named alpha, beta, delta, and theta. The slowest were delta rhythms at a frequency of 1 to 3 hertz, most prominent in deep sleep; theta rhythms have a frequency of 4 to 7 hertz, and are connected with mood; alpha rhythms run from 8 to 12 hertz, occurring most often in deep meditation; and beta rhythms, between 13 and 22 hertz, seemed to be confined to the frontal area of the brain where complex mental processes take place.

Young children have a tendency to react emotionally to frustration by acts of aggression linked with theta brain waves. It had also been discovered that those adults who were subject to uncontrolled fits of violent aggression often had dominant theta rhythms in their brain waves.

Dr. Grey Walter conjectured that this adjustment to frustration and disappointment was "one of the first and firmest foundations of personality," and went on to say:

"St. Augustine would have been interested in the measure in which EEG records confirm the connection between the sinful mood of the infant and the adult. Few of us indeed escape unscathed from the test. We are all miserable sinners. In ordinary circumstances the theta rhythms are scarcely visible in good-tempered adults, but they seem to be evoked even in them by a really disagreeable stimulus."

APPENDIX IV

In 1970 an experiment conducted in the state of Kansas, U.S.A., confirmed a revolutionary new medical theory that had been gaining currency for the previous few years—that many body functions thought to be involuntary could, in fact, be controlled. The experiment, conducted by Dr. Elmer Green, Director of the Menninger Foundation voluntary controls projects, was to attach EKG electrodes to the left hand and right ear of an Indian swami, while the swami stopped his own heart. Dr. Green thought the swami meant he was going to give himself some kind of neurological shock; but the shock the swami was talking about was psychological.

Before the self-induced shock the swami's recorded heart rate was smooth and even at seventy beats a minute. Suddenly, in the space of one beat, it jumped to almost three hundred beats per minute. The polygraph pens jumped up and down five times every second for a span of some seventeen seconds.

Animal experiments had shown that it was possible to teach rats to control their hearts, but the swami's experiment was the start of a series of experiments to teach humans to learn this technique to cure muscle tension, among other things. Out of this, and similar knowledge derived from the use of curare on rats, was developed the technique of "bio-feedback."

All learning requires feedback. When learning to speak, it is essential to hear. A child who is hard of hearing speaks poorly, but give him a hearing aid and he may learn to speak like a normal child.

So by its very nature, biofeedback implies the use of machines. A biofeedback machine is any device that makes a person more aware of a bodily function that he would be normally, and which the person uses in an attempt to control the function voluntarily. A stethoscope can be a biofeedback machine if a person uses it to learn what it feels like to have his heart-rate go up and down and to try to bring his heart under voluntary control.

Biofeedback, as a medical innovation, began in about 1958, the same year as Dr. Becker was starting his research into electrical stimulation and regeneration of bone tissue, and about the same time as the Chinese doctors were experimenting with a pulse stimulator for electro-acupuncture use in surgical operations.

But it was a Japanese psychologist, Dr. Joseph Kamiya—also in 1958—who, while studying EEG patterns, began to study in depth what the EEG was recording, what the brain was doing, and what the patient was verbally reporting he felt was happening. He had his subjects sit in a darkened room wired to the EEG and asked them to guess what state they were in: alpha or not alpha, A or B. By the third hour many of the subjects were guessing correctly three times out of four. However, the subjects found it difficult to describe the state, Kamiya said:

"The ineffability of the meditative state so often stressed in mystical writings is similar to statements many of my subjects made; for example: 'I can't describe this state...It has a certain feel about it...'; 'I feel calm...'; 'I feel stoned...'; 'I feel like I'm floating off the chair.' "

Unfortunately, biofeedback became the plaything of faddists and cultists and was claimed as the new panacea for everything, but in a few areas the findings have been of real significance. Some of biofeedback's greatest successes have been in relieving muscle tension. With special equipment that registers muscle activity with a tone, or a light, or electronic clicks, it is possible to learn to relax a muscle completely, or to isolate a single motor neuron and learn to "fire" it at will. Variations on this technique have been used to partially rehabilitate stroke victims, or to eliminate speech defects in slow readers, or to cure facial tics.

A much-publicized technique has been the use of "alpha-machines," which react to show that the user's brain-waves have entered the "alpha-state" of calm and relaxation. Brain-waves are a rough measure of mental activity; they are fastest during active, attentive thought, and slowest in deep sleep. Generally, stimulants such as caffeine, tobacco, and amphetamines speed up the predominant brain-waves, while alcohol, morphine, marijuana, and decreased blood sugar tend to slow them down.

Put simply, biofeedback is a technique for human self-monitoring in which a person is made conscious of his or her brain-waves while at the same time reflecting on his or her own state of mind; in other words, it is a mechanical device for presenting information externally about what is happening internally so that it may be analyzed objectively. The term biofeedback was defined by one of the pioneers, mathematician Robert Weiner, as "a method of controlling a system by re-inserting into it the result of its last performance."

With this control the patient can be instructed, among other things, to train himself to enter internal states of consciousness previously only possible to mystics, drug users, or cult initiates. But in less ecstatic circumstances biofeedback is being found a very effective therapy in pain clinics for migraine. This is done by means of "hand or finger-warming exercises."

In practice it is quite easy to learn how to raise the skin temperature of the hands or fingers by simply imagining that they are getting warmer. Soldiers serving in cold climates have been taught this technique. The rationale in migraine is that the headache is caused by dilation of extra- and intra-cranial arteries resulting from excessive autonomic nervous activity. Hand-warming is achieved by relaxation and hence a reduction of sympathetic activity.

But opponents of biofeedback fall back on that good old medical establishment objection to whatever is new, "the placebo effect," to explain such beneficial responses.

APPENDIX V

These observations led to another hypothesis: that the cerebellum is a modulator which arises to the needs of the organism. Cooper speculated, therefore, that chronic cerebellar stimulation leads to a build-up of chemical changes in neurotransmitter systems. If so, a possible eventual reconditioning or normalization of some abnormal brain functions mediated by chemical systems might take place during chronic stimulation of the cerebellar cortex.

APPENDIX VI

Another of our colleagues in the Tung Wah Hospital, Dr. K. Chau, my physician counterpart, had been experimenting by using the same methods in the treatment of status asthmaticus. He had found that it produced better results than any achieved by conventional therapy. The investigations were conducted from December 1972 to March 1973.

During this period, all thirty cases of bronchial asthma under the care of the medical unit of the Tung Wah Hospital were offered acupuncture and electro-stimulation therapy. Of the patients under observation, six had particularly severe bronchial asthma. They all had had recurrent attacks of severe status asthmaticus, a history of repeated hospital admissions for asthma within the past twelve months, and symptoms that interfered with work and sleep. In all six patients the asthmatic attacks were worse in winter. Four had associated emphysema. Three of them had been under the care of the unit for more than three consecutive years prior to the investigations and had previously received short-term corticosteroid therapy during approximately half of their hospital admissions because of poor response to other treatments. The other three patients had been treated previously in other hospitals, and had come into the unit as emergency cases with severe asthmatic attacks. One of them had continuous asthma for two months before being admitted. Dr. Chau also reported his findings in *The Asian Journal of Medicine:*

"All patients showed significant objective response to acupuncture and electro-stimulation therapy for mild to moderately severe asthma attacks, and also a significant improvement in the FEVI, FVC and PEFR after treatment... The results of the present study indicate that in the patients studied, acupuncture and electro-stimulation therapy is superior to conventional therapy in the management of severe bronchial asthma and status asthmaticus. It is superior in the aspects of potency of action, duration of effect, minimum of side effects, and absence of resistance to therapy..."[2]

APPENDIX VII

Since previous investigations had suggested that monoamines in the brain are especially important in analgesia, the Chinese scientists depleted the test rabbits of monoamines by administering the drug reserpine to block the effect of morphine as an analgesic. Surprisingly, it enhanced the effects of acupuncture. When the monoamines dopamine and 5-hydroxytryptamine were restored to the brain artificially, the effects of acupuncture analgesia returned to normal and morphine was again effective.

Conversely, when they similarly tested the effects of the neurotransmitter substance acetylcholine, they found that it played an important part in acupuncture analgesia. When acetylcholine action was blocked by atropine the effect of acupuncture was very much weakened. Morphine analgesia was not affected by interference with acetylcholine by intraventricular injection of atropine.

APPENDIX VIII

An American scientist, G. Dauth, reported that in his experimental cerebellar stimulation by implanted electrodes in cats he had concluded, in studying the effects of different frequencies, train durations and pulse durations, that there existed optimal values for each of these parameters— although an increase in pulse duration might compensate for a deficiency in train duration. He also reported that exceeding particular values may provide no greater benefit to the patient. He further suggested that progressively larger currents recruit progressively larger populations of neurons, yet warned against using excessive current application.[3]

Then two researchers, R. R. Myers and R. G. Bickford, demonstrated in both chloralose and sound-induced myoclonus in cats, that cerebellar stimulation at frequencies of 100-200 hertz clearly suppressed the myoclonus, whereas it was unaffected by stimulation at 1-10 hertz.[4]

APPENDIX IX

At first the plates were placed on the anterior lobe alone, because most of the experimental work concerned this area, which is the strongest inhibitor of seizure and motor activity. In certain patients, however, such as those with spasticity, the electrodes were placed only on the posterior lobe, which has strong connections with the motor cortex. Later, all new patients received stimulation of both lobes for better control. Bipolar stimulation between four or more pairs of electrodes was produced simultaneously.

All electrodes on each side were stimulated simultaneously. The current procedure was to stimulate the cerebellum continuously, but in two separate areas alternately. The units had an automatic timer. Stimulation was carried out with rectangular pulses, of 1 msec width, with a rate of 7 to 200 hertz, and an intensity of 0.5 to 14 volts. Generally speaking, epileptic patients received stimulation at 10 hertz and 10 volts, and spastic patients 200 hertz and 10 volts, depending on the condition of the patient.

APPENDIX X

One such experiment used 6-hydroxydopamine, which depresses catecholamine biosynthesis and destroys nerve terminals producing a catecholamine. When 6-hydroxydopamine was injected into the cisterna magna of the brains of six rats prepared for electrical stimulation, the rate at which the animals pressed the lever to obtain an electric "shock" in the medial forebrain bundle was roughly halved. A second injection virtually eliminated self-stimulation in five of the six rats.

Yet another experiment which indicated that noradrenaline is the catecholamine that excited the cerebral reward system of the rat was done with disulfiram and diethyldithiocarbamate. These drugs blocked the conversion of dopamine to noradrenaline. The inhibited self-stimulation of the animals was restored by injecting noradrenaline into a cerebral ventricle.

APPENDIX XI

Dr. L. S. Illis reported in *Nature:*

"Adult cats were anesthetized with intraperitoneal Nembutal. A catheter in the left ventricle was connected by a two-way tap to normal saline and fixation material. The left fifth lumbar root was exposed by enlarging the root foramen without disturbing the spinal cord dura mater, cardiac pace-maker electrodes were placed around the root and the root was stimulated with a 1 msec pulse, 300 cps, 2.5 volts...After stimulation of a single posterior root for 65 minutes, *changes were seen in the areas where monosynaptic fibres are known to terminate...*"[5] (my italics)

APPENDIX XII

In a personal communication with Dr. Becker regarding my own research, he said:

"I am enclosing a copy of the paper presented in France and also a preprint of our specific data on acupuncture. Neither of these is up to date and we are vigorously pursuing this line of investigation at the present time. Our additional data, not reflected in either manuscript, has been supportive of our original conception, and I believe at this time I can unequivocally state that there are significant electrical correlations for approximately 50 percent of the acupuncture points. We have concluded, therefore, that acupuncture has a basis in reality. Our concept as briefly outlined at the French Symposium is that there is a previously undescribed system of data transmission additional to the nerves in the living organism. We believe that this system is primitive in nature, operates with analog-type DC electrical signals and is concerned with the sensing of injury and effecting its control by healing processes. We believe the system is located in the perineural cells, Schwann cells peripherally and glia cells centrally. There is evidence at least in the glia that these cells are capable of controlling the operational levels of the nerve cells themselves. In this sense, then, the system becomes analogous to a hybrid computer: that is, with a basic analog system and a superimposed high-speed digital system. Since the primary input to the system is the sensing of injury, we postulate that this system, at least in part, carries the pain sensation. Since our data indicate that the system is electronic in nature, and carries messages by means of extremely small currents, the insertion of needles could well produce significant perturbation. Of course, one can theoretically optimize the effect by the direct injection of electrical current."

APPENDIX XIII

Even microinjections of local anesthetic into this same area were ineffective in raising the pain threshold; in fact they made the tested animal more sensitive to pain.[6,7] Researchers observed that the analgesic effect in animals outlasted brain stimulation from a few minutes to several hours, depending on the duration and intensity of the stimulation;[8] in humans the effect lasted up to twenty-four hours after stopping the stimulation.[9]

It was deduced that stimulation-produced analgesia, like acupuncture, appeared to be modulated by monoaminergic transmission, facilitated by serotonin and dopamine, and antagonized by noradrenaline.[10,11] Morphine had comparable pharmacological susceptibilities and one noted research scientist suggested that they must both depend, at least in part, upon a common neural substrate. It was also significant that opiate receptor binding sites were found in areas in the brain-stem where SPA was most effective.[12]

APPENDIX XIV

In pain relief, stimulation of the intralaminar nuclei was analgesic if it remained at low frequency and low amplitude; but increasing the frequency or the amplitude caused arousal, anxiety, and a need to escape, and the pain relief was than totally masked by these emotions. On the other hand, low-level stimulation produced a feeling of relaxation and well-being.[13]

In another demonstration of the importance of frequency cats were trained to discriminate between two different repetition rates of light-flicker or click. Subsequently, electrodes were implanted in the brain reticular formation, and with bursts of electrical pulses at the same two repetition rates significant levels of discriminated performance were obtained in all cats very quickly. The memory of what had been learned was to be found in the unique cell-firing rhythm of the brain.[14,15]

APPENDIX XV

It is interesting to reflect further on the use of the term *logos* in bringing back an individual to a spiritual center. The concept of the *logos* in the Judaic-Christian and Greek classical sense has played a profound part in the development of Western civilization, but there is also a significant parallel in the recent transformation of Chinese society through Chairman Mao Zedong's definition of the generic Chinese word *szuh-siang*, meaning "correct thinking."[16]

Logos, as Frankl says, is a Greek word, but the concept behind it is rooted in Judaic-Greek etymology. To the Jews, *logos,* "the word," was not merely a sound but a dynamic force, the *Word* of God by which he created the world, the very idea of the action of God, the creative and illuminating power of God enabling the object of its interest to accomplish his purpose. To the Greeks, *logos* was the *reason* of God, the principle of order under which the universe continued to exist; a purpose, a plan, a design, the mind of God controlling the world and every man and woman in it. It was the combination of these two streams of thought that gave to the Apostle John his conception of Jesus Christ as "the Word of God made flesh," the unique revelation of Christianity.

But, taking up Frankl's point that logotherapy—as he uses the term and technique—is not necessarily religious, but is integrally related to the human dimension and aspiration, as indicated above, it is fascinating to study the similar technique developed and practiced in China by the late Chairman Mao. His uniquely personal form of "spiritual" Marxism was used to transform a nation of some 800 million inhabitants disillusioned and despairing over the lack of meaning in their lives, to forge them into a people with vision, values, and meaning. In order to create such a "new society," with "new men" and "new women," he had to create a new form of revolution—which he did through what is now known world-wide as "Maoism." While Western intellectuals nibbled peripherally at the problems confronting a dying Western society and their possible solutions, falling back defeated into reductionism and nihilism, Chairman Mao was switching his almost one-billion (one-third-of-the-world) nation from being one of the world's most drug-addicted, despairing, and defeated societies to being the greatest cult-addicted but vital society by means of a psychospiritual process. Earlier, Hitler had achieved something similar with "Nazism," his hybrid amalgam of vision, values, and meaning in "National

Socialism," which transformed Germany. Obviously, these were perversions of a process inherent in humankind and society which could be harnessed to higher goals.

In the first two decades of the twentieth century in China, doubt and uncertainty—the twin constituent elements in the condition of anxiety—had replaced the traditional pride and confidence. Chinese intellectuals then turned to the West in search of its apparently successful ideas, and discovered the materialist Marxism so alien to its own history and traditions. Like personal doubts and uncertainties, group or national doubts and uncertainties regarding the viability of social structures, once they are successfully challenged, operate in similar fashion in that they empty the system of existing values and ideas leaving hopelessness, disillusion, and despair. When it is seen that the previous ideas and values no longer accurately articulate the human situation, they become increasingly destructive and are powerless to solve the human situation, in the West in this century (this is evident in the collapse of the ecclesiastical symbols of Christianity, the political symbols of democracy, and the ideological symbols of Marxism.)

China had tried institutionalized democracy, and ecclesiastical Christianity. Both had failed because they were already failing in the West. But Marxism was still relatively new in the early 1920s, and the debate in China centered around whether Marxism's developing institutional form in Soviet Russia was applicable to China, or whether its earlier dynamic ideas and values as articulated by the young Marx and adapted to China were more relevant. China's intellectuals chose the latter, which evolved into Maoism.

The Maoist vision was both particular and universal. Particular in that the People's Republic of China was seen as the spiritual center and source of inspiration and the example for people's liberation movements everywhere; universal in that it postulated a giant moral battle on a global scale between the forces of good and the forces of evil, while that same moral struggle took place in the life of each individual. It was also intensely evangelistic and, as a consequence, became messianic and eschatological, deifying Mao in the present and envisioning a new, utopian age through Maoist principles of world revolution.

The transformation of men and women, from being "self-centered" to being "others-centered" was fundamental to the success of the whole revolution, and in this conception and campaign Mao not only matched the young idealist Marx, but surpassed him and other Marxist leaders.

Self interest was the original sin of the Maoist spiritual concepts. In study sessions throughout the country all students and teachers had to practice "self-criticism," confess "self-interest," and "thoroughly destroy self-interest" in order to uphold the concept of "teaching for revolution and learning for revolution." It was self-interest, Mao said, which produced careerism, individualism, elitism, avarice, profiteering, pursuit of fame, and privilege. Within a few years the majority of Chinese were convinced that salvation through "struggle-criticism-transformation" was readily if laboriously possible, because they had seen the conversion process work. Mao's "Thought" was said to generate *szu-hsiang,* meaning "correct thought," and this was the determinant of all action," translating doctrine into reality, and sustaining people's faith in the darkest hour."

Despite its dramatic impact it was evident that Maoism was inadequate to meet China's needs; its demonstrable weakness confirmed the axiom that "a spiritual center," or spiritual corpus, cannot be produced at will simply to support a political or cultural system; it has to be the mainspring, the inspiration, of such a system, rising from the people upwards and not descending from the authorities downwards. Without such an inspirational spiritual center, or corpus, there is an inevitable separation, a lack of integration, from the whole of reality, an isolation of the individual self, a sense of non-identity with or non-participation in cosmic or divine purpose.

The dissatisfied individuals then tend to break away from the less concerned mass and form smaller, then larger, groups in order to identify themselves with something supra-or trans-individual. This helps to alleviate their sense of alienation, emptiness, and meaninglessness by accepting another imposed authority in place of the weak or inadequate father, or parents, or government, or church; surrendering their freedom to question, finding solutions for their immediate problems in uncritically accepting strongly affirmed answers to vaguely postulated and usually specious questions. In order to allay the increasing pangs of anxiety brought on by the increasing emptiness and meaninglessness as they move from one idiosyncratic group to another, these individuals or groups eventually retreat from challenging freedom to a robotomorphic situation which discourages disturbing questions and encourages packaged answers.

APPENDIX XVI

Dr. Viktor E. Frankl is a distinguished professor of "logotherapy" at the United States International University, San Diego, and visiting clinical professor at Stanford University, whose book, *Man's Search for Meaning*—among twenty-seven others—the *American Journal of Psychiatry* has called "...perhaps the most significant thinking since Freud and Adler."

Dr. Frankl has stated emphatically that the psychoanalyst who, in unmasking the motives of a patient, does not stop when he is finally confronted with what is authentic and genuine within the patient's own psyche, "is really unmasking his own cynical attitude, his own nihilistic tendency to devalue and depreciate that which is human in man."[17]

Frankl has done more than anyone to investigate and elucidate the problems of twentieth century emptiness and meaninglessness since he faced them at the door of the gas ovens of Auschwitz during World War II. He has classified this "sense of despair over the lack of a meaning in life" as "noögenic neurosis," a new syndrome of twentieth century society. Noögenic (from the Greek *noos,* meaning "mind") neuroses have their origin not in the psychological but rather in the noölogical dimension of human experience, and is caused by "existential frustration." This is experienced when man's will-to-meaning is frustrated. Because existence itself is the specifically human mode of being, the striving to find a concrete meaning in personal existence is the *will* to meaning, and when this is frustrated it results in noögenic rather than psychogenic neurosis. Having defined it, Dr. Frankl has postulated and practiced a new method of treatment which he has called "logotherapy." Describing this therapy he says:

"*Logos* is a Greek word that denoted 'meaning.' Logotherapy, or, as it has been called by some authors 'the Third Viennese School of Psychotherapy,' focuses on the meaning of human existence as well as on man's search for such a meaning. According to logotherapy, the striving to find a meaning in one's life is the primary motivational force in man. That is why I speak of a *will-to-meaning* in contrast to the pleasure principle (or, as we would term it, the *will-to-pleasure*) on which Freudian psychiatry is centered, as well as in contrast to the *will-to-power* stressed by Adlerian psychology."[18]

Frankl goes on to explain that while in psychoanalysis the patient must tell his therapist things that are sometimes difficult to tell, in logotherapy the patient must hear things that are sometimes disagreeable to hear. He demonstrates that despair over the meaning of life is a very real neurosis, and just as sexual frustration may lead to neuroses, the frustration of the will-to-meaning may also lead to neuroses. However, noögenic neuroses do not emerge from conflicts between drives and instincts, but rather from conflicts between various values; in other words, from moral conflicts or spiritual problems.

Logotherapy, therefore, aims at breaking up the typical self-centeredness of the neurotic—or, as we are discussing from our experience, the addict—instead of continually fostering and reinforcing it, as is the usual practice. It focuses on assignments and meanings to be fulfilled by the patient in his future. It considers the individual as a being whose main concern consists of fulfilling a meaning and in actualizing values, rather than in mere gratification of instincts, mere reconciliation of the conflicting claims of id, ego and superego, or mere adaption and adjustment to society and personal environment. Men and women, in contrast to lesser animals, must have a goal in life. Frankl asserts:

"A goal can be a goal in life, however, only if it has meaning. Now I am prepared for the argument that psychotherapy belongs to the realm of science and is not concerned with values; but I believe there is no such thing as psychotherapy unconcerned with values, only one that is blind to values. A psychotherapy which not only recognised man's spirit, but actually starts from it, may be termed *logotherapy.* In this connection, *logos* is intended to signify 'the spiritual' and beyond that 'the meaning.' (It must be kept in mind, however, that within the framework of logotherapy 'spiritual' does not have a religious connotation but refers to the specifically human dimension)."

Frankl points out that it is not the aim of logotherapy to take the place of existing psychotherapy, but only to complement it, thereby forming a picture of men and women in their wholeness, which must include the spiritual dimension. Psychotherapy, he argues, as it has been developed up until the present, needs to be supplemented by a procedure which operates beyond the field of the Oedipus complex and the inferiority complex, or, in more general terms, beyond all affect-dynamics:

"What is still missing," he declares, "is a form of psychotherapy which gets underneath psycho-dynamics, which sees beneath the psychic malaise of the neurotic, his spiritual struggles... What we are concerned with is a psychotherapy in spiritual terms..."

APPENDIX XVII

Summary of follow-up of patients treated in England from October 1973 to December 1980

1. Type of addiction:

drugs (legal and illegal) 130
alcohol 30
cigarettes 26

(Note: Patients treated by NET for conditions other than the above are *not* included in this survey.)

2. Years of using the addictive substance daily:

½-1 year 8%
2-4 years 30%
5-10 years 40%
11-20 years 15%
21-30 years 4%
Over 30 years 3%

(Majority of drug-addicts were main-liners who injected the drug into a vein.)

3. Amount of daily drug use on admission for NET:

Slight (within the maximum 23%
prescribable limit for drugs)
Moderate 37%
Heavy 26%
Extremely heavy 14%

These daily amounts ranged from 300 mg prescribed heroin to 10 g street heroin (officially up to 40% purity in London in 1980); cocaine: ½-10 g; methadone: 40–800 mg. Various narcotic or psychotropic drugs: up to 70 tablets daily (*All* drugs were stopped totally and immediately on commencing NET.)

4. Patient drop-out rate over seven years of those who began NET but did not complete five days of detoxification: 1.6% (Compare with published figures in U.S.A. and U.K. of other treatment modalities: from 45% to 75% to 90% drop-out rate.[19,20,21])

5. Summary of information received from postal questionnaires (multiple outcome variables) or direct reporting for NET follow-up 1 to 8 years after treatment (return rate—50%):

80% were drug free.
(Others have been reported drug free since the review was completed.)

78% were alcohol free.
(An additional 7 alcoholics whose goal on admission was controlled drinking all reported success.)

44% were cigarette free.
(U.S. figures indicate that "when effectiveness is defined in terms of heroin or methadone abstinence, *less than 10%* are judged successful 10 years after treatment."[22])

60% were less than 30 years old.

65% had less than 2 weeks or no "rehabilitation" at all after their 10 days of NET;
the average length of stay in "rehab" for all NET patients was *16 days.* (In other programs, "success" depended on the length of time in the program, usually *18 months* or longer.[23])

67% reported decreased use of alcohol, cigarettes and/or marijuana.

75% reported improved sleep.

87% reported improved health.

77% had never made alcohol a substitute dependence

23% had temporarily made alcohol a substitute dependence (though drug-free)

0% were dependent on alcohol at the time of the questionnaire
(Compare U.S. government figures published in 1982: 60% of those treated became heavy or very heavy drinkers.[24])

68% rarely feel a craving for the drug, alcohol, or cigarette (though drug-free)

15% occasionally feel a craving for the drug, alcohol, or cigarette (though drug-free)

17% frequently feel a craving for the drug, alcohol, or cigarette (though drug-free)

6. Statistical report of those who became re-addicted:

78% were using less of their substance of abuse than before NET.

44% reported improved health.

64% reported improved relationships with spouse/family.

50% were more able to cope with daily problems.

All drug addicts including the recidivists, had diminished their alcohol intake.

APPENDIX XVIII

Withdrawal

When withdrawn from a user, every psychoactive drug appears, after daily use even for periods as short as one week, to cause a withdrawal or abstinence syndrome (AS).[25,26]

Apart from opioid withdrawal, the AS may be mild enough to be imperceptible to the physician and cause no complaint by the patient. In addition, there is variation in the severity of the AS in different patients using the same dosage of the same drug. Some who try to withdraw from Valium, for example, experience symptoms as severe as the worst opioid withdrawal; their Chronic Withdrawal Syndrome (CWS) may last as long (or longer) after Valium as it does after methadone withdrawal. A physician, alcoholic for only three years, reported recently in the *British Medical Journal* that after stopping drinking completely, "it was two years before memory fully returned and rational thinking approached normality."[27]

The typical AS for some of the main drugs of abuse are recorded as reported in medical literature.

1) *Opioids* including codeine, Demerol (meperidine or pethidine in U.K.), Percodan (oxycodone); Darvon (propoxyphene—Doloxene in U.K.), Talwin (pentazocine or Fortral in U.K.) etc. (listed in order of severity of symptoms): Craving for the drug of abuse, anxiety, "yen" sleep, yawning, rubbing nose, rhinorrhea, lacrimation, perspiration, bone and muscle aches, crossing and uncrossing of legs, muscle twitches, hot or cold flashes, anorexia, gooseflesh, dilated pupils, restlessness, nausea, shivering, stomach cramps, febrile facies, vomiting, diarrhea, insomnia, increases in respiratory rate, blood pressure (BP), temperature, blood sugar, basal metabolic rate; loss of weight.[28]

The Chronic (or Protracted) Withdrawal Syndrome is characterized by a modest decrease in BP, pulse rate, body temperature; feelings of weakness, apathy, tiredness, social withdrawal, dysphoria. These symptoms persist for at least six months following withdrawal.[29] After methadone withdrawal, it has been reported that the CWS may last for as long as one-and-a-half years.[30]

2) *Alcohol:* Somatic: tremor, muscle jerks, hyperreflexia. Autonomic: BP increase, heart rate increase, hyperventilation, anorexia, nausea and vomiting, diarrhea, diaphoresis, fever. Sleep: insomnia (delayed onset and disturbed quality), nightmares. Seizures: major, minor. Sensory: pain, pruritis, visual disturbances, paresthesias. Affective: anxiety, mania, depression. Sensorium and Orientation: agitation, disorientation, delusions, hallucinations.[31]

3) *Barbiturates and related hypnotics* such as Seconal, Tuinal, Doriden (glutethimide), Placidyl (ethchlorvynol), Quaalude (methaqualone—Mandrax in U.K.) etc: Symptoms commence twelve to sixteen hours after the last dose, with anxiety and weakness. After twenty-four hours, a fall in BP with faintness on standing; tremulousness, restlessness, muscular fasciculations, anorexia, vomiting, abdominal distress, mydriasis, hyperreflexia, insomnia, weight loss, an increased startle response to auditory or visual stimuli. Generalized convulsions (which may occur from the sixteenth hour till as late as the eighth day); the incidence is 75 percent in those using over 900 mg of barbiturate per day for over one month.[32] Re-

versible psychosis, marked by agitation, insomnia, disorientation in time and place, delusions, auditory and visual hallucinations, elevated temperature, rapid pulse rate, exhaustion. Death can occur.[33] Sleep problems can persist for four months.[34]

4) Tranquilizers and *Anxiolytics* such as Valium, Librium, Heminevrin (chlormethiazole—widely used in U.K. for alcohol withdrawal) etc: severe insomnia, tension, restlessness, anxiety, extreme dysphoria, panic attacks, hand tremor, profuse sweating, palpitations, faintness, difficulty in concentrating, nausea, dry retching, vomiting, weight loss, blurring of vision, difficulty in focusing, persistent headache and/or head throbbing, muscle pains and "stiffness," muscle twitching, intolerance to light and sound, sensory changes for touch, noise, vision and smell, unsteadiness and a feeling of motion, perceptual disturbance, depersonalization and derealization, psychotic reactions, epileptic seizures (a 2.5 percent incidence recorded among forty patients who had been using 10 mg diazepam or 4 mg lorazepam daily for four months or longer).[35,36,37]

5) Antidepressants, tricyclic such as Tofranil (imipramine) or MAO inhibitors such as Parnate (tranylcypromine): acute anxiety, restlessness, weakness, nausea, vomiting, diarrhea, dizziness, disorientation, headaches, confusion, hallucinations, psychosis. Symptoms may persist for several months.[38,39,40] Persistent convulsions have been reported in infants born to mothers under treatment with clomipramine (Anafranil).[41]

6) Psychedelics (or hallucinogens) such as PCP or "angel dust" (phencyclidine), LSD, hashish, marijuana: PCP AS causes extreme craving, anergia, short- or long-term depression, anxiety, physical discomfort, tremor, insomnia.[42,43] Marijuana: Sleep disturbance, irritability, restlessness, decreased appetite, sweating, sudden weight loss.[44]

7) Stimulants such as cocaine, amphetamines, Ritalin (methylphenidate), Preludin (phenmetrazine): a marked "let-down" effect, extreme fatigue, lengthy sleep, increased appetite, acute depression.[45] The feelings of apathy, inadequacy and depression may wax and wane over several months.[46] N.B: After repeated treatment of rhesus monkeys with high doses of I.V. methamphetamine, the levels of norepinephrine and dopamine in the brain remained markedly reduced for up to six months after the methamphetamine was discontinued.[47]

8) Inhalants such as solvents and glue: psychological dependence occurs regularly but physical dependence is thought to be mild. AS gives fine tremors, irritability, anxiety, insomnia, tingling and cramps of hands and feet, aggressiveness, vertigo, nausea, anorexia, D.T.'s.[48]

9) Nicotine (cigarettes, chewing tobacco): irritability, sleepiness, hunger, tenseness, malaise, craving, increase in BP and pulse rate.[49]

Note: Two symptoms which occur in withdrawal from every group of psychoactive drugs are *craving for the substance,* and *anxiety.* Special attention was paid to the effects of NET on these symptoms. The results are detailed in Figure 7 in Appendix XIX.

APPENDIX XIX

For all patients treated by NET in the period January to December 1980 for all addictions combined ($n = 102$), quantitative estimates of the nineteen "Abstinence Syndrome" (AS) Indicators used by C.K. Himmelsbach [28] were made by the nursing staff four times daily. Each of the nineteen signs and symptoms was recorded on a 0-4 point scale, totaling a possible 76 points. No patient was graded 4 (the worst) in every indicator simultaneously and the dominant AS indicators varied from patient to patient. Since all drugs were totally stopped on admission, and NET was begun immediately, withdrawal symptomology was kept at a minimum. This is shown in Figure 5 (see next page), which also lists Himmelsbach's AS indicators. The graph shows the mean of daily means of the AS for all addictions treated by NET in 1980, the highest mean recorded being 9 points out of the possible 76. That is, NET was remarkably successful at reducing withdrawal symptoms even without any supportive drugs being administered.

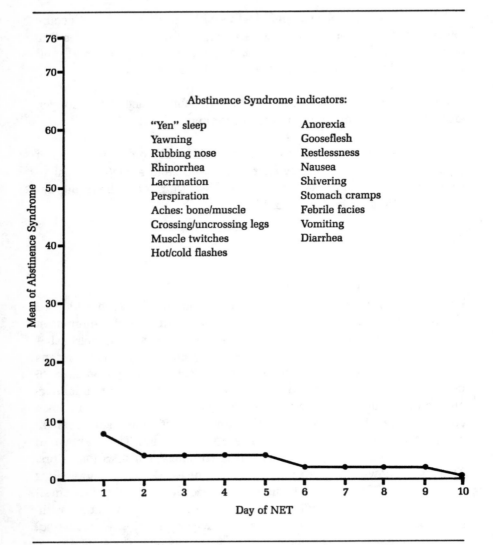

Figure 5. Reduction of withdrawal symptoms in patients treated by NET, without any supportive drugs, based on Himmelsbach's Abstinence Syndrome (AS).

All patients were initially skeptical of NET's ability to prevent their suffering during the withdrawal period. When recidivist patients undergo a second treatment they have the confidence of knowing of NET's previous effectiveness. Figure 6 shows that for ten patients treated twice, the symptoms of withdrawal were diminished even more the second time.

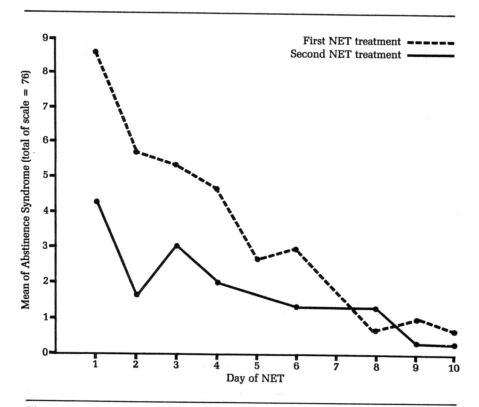

Figure 6. Comparison of the AS for 10 subjects for first and second treatments on NET. The vertical axis has been shortened from 76 points (as in figure 5) to 9 points to highlight the differences between reactions to the first and second treatments.

Craving, anxiety, and lethargy are three withdrawal symptoms that are not alleviated by any form of withdrawal treatment other than NET. Figure 7 illustrates the effects of NET on craving and anxiety. Recordings were made four times daily on days 1-5 and twice daily on days 6-10. In each condition, 4 represents the maximum of the symptom and 0 the least.

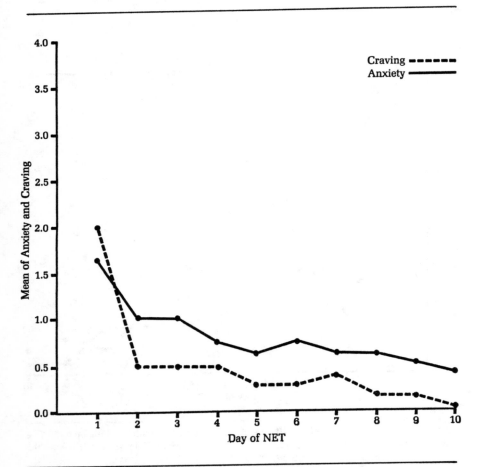

Figure 7. Mean of daily means for each subject for craving and anxiety (n = 102).

NOTES

1: Addicts and NET

1. US Government pamphlet. Why people smoke cigarettes. Los Angeles Times 1983 March 7:Part I, 5(cols 5-6).
2. Masi D (interview). Drugs cost industry $25 billion each year. USA Today 1983 March 10:11A(cols 1-7).
3. Nicholi AM. The nontherapeutic use of psychoactive drugs. A modern epidemic. N Engl J Med 1983;308:925-33.
4. Eady B. Kids, drugs and alcohol. USA Today 1983 April 25:1A(cols 6-7).
5. Roberts JL. Campus binge. Wall Street Journal 1983 Feb 8:1(col 1), 21(cols 1-3).
6. Demarest M. Cocaine: middle class high. Time 1981 July 6:56-63.
7. Andersen K. Crashing on cocaine. Time 1983 April 11:22-31.
8. De Leon G. The role of rehabilitation. In: Nahas GG, Frick HC, eds. Drug abuse in the modern world. A perspective for the eighties. New York: Pergamon Press, 1981:298-307.

2: Introduction to Addictions

1. Acupuncture Anaesthesia. Peking: Foreign Languages Press, 1973.
2. Wint Guy, ed. Asia Handbook. London: Blond and Briggs, 1965. London: Penguin Books, 1969.
3. Wint Guy. The Third Killer. London: Chatto and Windus, 1965.
4. Cooper IS, Riklan M. Snider RS, eds. The Cerebellum, Epilepsy and Behavior. New York: Plenum Press, 1974.

3: "Walking on Both Feet"

1. Mann Felix. Acupuncture: Cure of Many Diseases. London: William Heinemann Medical Books, 1972.
2. Liberation Daily News 1972 Jan 22.
3. Limoge A, Debras C, Coeytaux R, Cara M. Electrical technique for electropharmaceutical anaesthesia concerning 300 operations. In: Wageneder FM, Germann RH, eds. Electrotherapeutic Sleep and Electroanaesthesia. Graz: RM Verlag, 1975
4. Wall PD, Sweet WH. Temporary abolition of pain in man. Science 1967; 155:108-9.
5. Sweet WH, Wespic JG. Treatment of chronic pain by stimulation of fibres of primary afferent neurons. Trans-America Neural Association 1968; 93:103-7.
6. Nathan PW, Wall PD. Treatment of postherpetic neuralgia by prolonged electric stimulation. Br Med J 1974;3:645-7.
7. Walter W Grey. The Living Brain. London: Duckworth and Company, 1946.
8. Cooper IS, Riklan M, Snider RS, eds. The Cerebellum, Epilepsy and Behavior. New York: Plenum Press, 1974:119-71.

4: From Surgery to Research

1. Wen HL, Cheung SY. Treatment of drug addiction by acupuncture and electrical stimulation. Asian J Med 1973;9:138-41.
2. Research Group of Acupuncture Anaesthesia, Peking Medical College. The role of some neurotransmitters of brain in finger-acupuncture analgesia. Scientia Sinica 1974;17:112-30.
3. Science Report. The Times (London) 1974 March 28.
4. Mayer DJ. Pain inhibition by electrical brain stimulation: comparison to morphine. Neurosci Res Prog Bull 1975;13:94-100.
5. Cooper IS, Riklan M, Snider S, eds. The Cerebellum, Epilepsy and Behavior. New York: Plenum Press, 1974: 119-71.
6. Collier HOJ. The experimental analysis of drug dependence. ICI (Imperial Chemical Industries) 1972 Sep.
7. Pert CB, Snyder SH. Opiate receptor: demonstration in nervous tissue. Science 1973;179:1011-4.
8. Anonymous. Electrical stimulation of the brain (Editorial). Lancet 1974;ii: 562-4.

9. Becker RO. Electromagnetic forces and life processes. Technology Rev 1972;75:2-8.
10. Becker RO. The basic biological data transmission and control system influenced by electrical forces. Ann NY Acad Sci 1974;238:236-41.

5: Initial Development of NET

1. Becker RO, Marino AA. Electromagnetism and Life. Albany: State University of New York Press, 1982:14-7.
2. Patterson MA. Electro-acupuncture in alcohol and drug addictions. Clin Med 1974;81:9-13.
3. Hughes J. Isolation of an endogenous compound from the brain with pharmacological properties similar to morphine. Brain Res 1975;88:295-306.
4. Terenius L, Wahlström A. Search for an endogenous ligand for the opiate receptor. Acta Physiol Scand 1975;94:74-81.
5. Pasternak GW, Goodman R, Snyder SH. An endogenous morphine-like factor in mammalian brain. Life Sci 1975; 16:1765-9.
6. Smyth DK. Morphine-like peptides in the brain. Sandoz Foundation Lecture, Institute of Neurology, London, 1976.
7. Bloom F, Segal D, Ling N, Guillemin R. Endorphins: profound behavioral effects in rats suggest new etiological factors in mental illness. Science 1976;194:630-2.
8. Kosterlitz HW, Hughes J. Some thoughts on the significance of enkephalin, the endogenous ligand. Life Sci 1975;17:91-6.
9. Hughes J. Enkephalin and drug dependence. Br J Addiction 1976;71:199-209.
10. Melzack R. The Puzzle of Pain. New York: Basic Books Inc, 1973.
11. Giesler GJ, Liebeskind JC. Inhibition of visceral pain by electrical stimulation of the periaqueductal grey matter. Pain 1976;2:43-8.
12. Liebeskind JC, Guilbaud G, Besson JM, Oliveras JL. Analgesia from electrical stimulation of the periaqueductal grey matter in the cat: behavioral observations and inhibitory effects on spinal cord interneurons. Brain Res 1973;50:441-6.
13. Goodman SJ, Holcombe V. Paper given at First World Congress on Pain, Florence, Italy, 1975.
14. Liebeskind JC, Giesler GJ, Urca G. Evidence pertaining to an endogenous mechanism of pain inhibition in the central nervous system. In: Zotterman Y, ed. Sensory functions of the skin in primates, with special reference to man. Oxford: Pergamon Press, 1976.
15. Mayer DJ, Wolffe TL, Akil H, Carder B, Liebeskind JC. Analgesia from electrical stimulation in the brainstem of the rat. Science 1971;174:1351-4.
16. Mayer DJ. Pain inhibition by electrical brain stimulation: comparison to morphine. Neurosci Res Prog Bull 1975;13:94-100.
17. Liebeskind JC, Guilbaud G, Besson JM, Oliveras JL. Analgesia from electrical stimulation of the periaqueductal grey matter in the cat: behavioral observations and inhibitory effects on spinal cord interneurons. Brain Res 1973;50:441-6.
18. Akil H, Mayer DJ. Antagonism of stimulation-produced analgesia by p-CPA, a serotonin synthesis inhibitor. Brain Res 1972;44:692-7.
19. Liebman JM, Mayer DJ, Liebeskind JC. Mesencephalic central grey lesions and fear-motivated behavior in rats. Brain Res 1970;23:353-70.
20. Mayer DJ, Wolffe TL, Akil H, Carder B, Liebeskind JC. Analgesia from electrical stimulation in the brainstem of the rat. Science 1971;174:1351-4.
21. Oliveras JL, Redjemi F, Guilbaud G, Besson JM. Analgesia induced by electrical stimulation of the inferior centralis nucleus of the raphe in the cat. Pain 1975;1:139-45.
22. Liebeskind JC, Giesler GJ, Urca G. Evidence pertaining to an endogenous mechanism of pain inhibition in the central nervous system. In: Zotterman Y, ed. Sensory functions of the skin in primates, with special reference to man. Oxford: Pergamon Press, 1976.
23. Hughes J. Isolation of an endogenous compound from the brain with pharmacological properties similar to morphine. Brain Res 1975;88:295-306.

24. Hughes J, Smith TW, Morgan B, Fothergill L. Purification and properties of enkephalin—the possible endogenous ligand for the morphine receptor. Life Sci 1975;16:1753-8.

25. Akil H, Mayer DJ, Liebeskind JC. Antagonism of stimulation-produced analgesia by naloxone, a narcotic antagonist. Science 1976;191:961-2.

26. Adams JE. Naloxone reversal of analgesia produced by brain stimulation in the human. Pain 1976;2:161-6.

27. Goldstein A, Hilgard ER. Failure of the opiate antagonist naloxone to modify hypnotic analgesia. Proc Nat Acad Sci 1975; 72:2041-5.

28. Hughes J. Enkephalin and drug dependence. Br J Addiction 1976;71:199-209.

29. Ng LKY, Douthitt TO, Thoa NB, Albert CA. Modification of morphine-withdrawal syndrome in rats following transauricular electrostimulation: an experimental paradigm for auricular electroacupuncture. Biolog Psychiat 1975;10:575-80.

30. Dymond AM, Coger RW, Serafetinides EA. Intracerebral current levels in man during electro-sleep therapy. Biolog Psychiat 1975;10:101-4.

31. Braestrup C, Nielsen M, Olsen CE. Urinary and brain β-carboline-3-carboxylates as potent inhibitors of brain benzodiazepine receptors. Proc Natl Acad Sci 1980;77:2288-92.

32. Altura BT, Altura BM. Phencyclidine, lysergic acid diethylamide and mescaline: cerebral artery spasms and hallucinogenic activity. Science 1981; 212:1051-2.

6: The Importance of Frequencies

1. Patterson MA. Acupuncture and neuroelectric therapy in the treatment of drug and alcohol addictions. Aust J Alc Drug Dependence 1975;2:90-5.

2. Alexander P, Hamilton Fairley G, Smithers DW. Repeated acupuncture and serum hepatitis. Br Med J 1974;2:466.

3. Patterson MA. Addictions Can Be Cured. Berkhamsted, England: Lion Publishing, 1975:92.

4. Wagner MS. Getting the health out of people's daily lives. Lancet 1982;ii: 1207-8.

5. Capel ID, Pinnock MH, Withey NJ, Williams DC, Patterson MA. The effect of electrostimulation on barbiturate-induced sleeping times in rats. Drug Dev Res 1982;2:73-9.

6. Capel ID, Pinnock MH, Patterson MA. The influence of electrostimulation on hexobarbital induced loss of righting reflex in rats. Acupuncture and Electro-Therapeutics Res, Int J 1982;7:17-26.

7. Anonymous. Clonidine for opiate withdrawal (Editorial comment). Lancet 1980;ii:649.

8. Gold MS, Pottash AC, Sweeney DR, Kleber HD, Redmond DE. Rapid opiate detoxification: clinical evidence of antidepressant and antipanic effects of opiates. Am J Psychiatry 1979;136:982-3.

9. Gold MS, Pottash AC. Endorphins, locus coeruleus, clonidine and lofexidine; a mechanism for opiate withdrawal and new nonopiate treatments. Advances in Alcohol and Substance Abuse 1981;1:33-52.

10. Charney DS, Sternberg DE, Kleber HD, Heninger GR, Redmond DE. The clinical use of clonidine in abrupt withdrawal from methadone. Arch Gen Psychiatry 1981;38:1273-7.

11. Washton AM, Resnick RB. Clonidine in opiate withdrawal: review and appraisal of clinical findings. Pharmacotherapy 1981;1:140-6.

12. Meyer F. Evidence before hearing of California State Senate Health Committee. The Journal (The Addiction Research Foundation of Ontario) 1977 March 1:6(3),5.

13. Trocchi Alex. Cain's Book. New York: Grove Press, 1960.

14. Cooper IS, Riklan M, Snider RS, eds. The Cerebellum, Epilepsy and Behavior. New York: Plenum Press, 1974.

15. Becker RO. The basic biological data transmission and control system influenced by electrical forces. Ann NY Acad Sci 1974;238:236-41.

16. Friedenberg ZB, Brighton CT. Electrical fracture healing. Ann NY Acad Sci 1974;238:564-74.

17. Rowley BA, McKenna JM, Chase GR, Wolcott LE. The influence of electrical

current on an infecting microorganism in wounds. Ann NY Acad Sci 1974;238:543-51.

18. Cara M, Debras C, Dufour B, Limoge A. Long-term electro-medical anaesthesia in forty cases of major urological surgery. In: Wageneder FM, Germann RH, eds. Electrotherapeutic Sleep and Electroanaesthesia. Vol III. Third International Symposium in Varna. Graz: R M Verlag, 1974.

19. Long DM, Hagfors N. Electrical stimulation in the nervous system: the current status of electrical stimulation of the nervous system for relief of pain. Brain 1975;1:109-23.

20. Fox EJ, Melzack R. Transcutaneous electrical stimulation and acupuncture: comparison of treatment for low-back pain. Pain 1976;2:141-8.

21. Melzack R, Stillwell DM, Fox EJ. Trigger points and acupuncture points for pain: correlations and implications. Pain 1977;3:3-23.

22. Godec C, Cass AS, Ayala GF. Electrical stimulation for incontinence. Technique, selection and results. Urology 1976;7:388-97.

23. Cook AW, Weinstein SP. Chronic dorsal column stimulation in M.S. NY State J Med 1973 Dec 15:2868-72.

24. Illis LS, Sedgwick EM, Oygar AE, Sabbahi Awadalla MA. Dorsal-column stimulation in the rehabilitation of patients with multiple sclerosis. Lancet 1976;i:1383-6.

25. Frederickson RCA. Morphine withdrawal response and central cholinergic activity. Nature 1975;257:131-2.

26. Banshchikov VM, Sudakov HV, Kulikova YI, Arsentyev DA. Behavioural and electroencephalographic responses in a state of electrically induced sleep, In: Wageneder FM, Germann RH, eds. Electrotherapeutic Sleep and Electroanaesthesia. Vol III. Third International Symposium in Varna. Graz: R M Verlag, 1974.

27. Stadelmayr-Maiyores HG. Technique of electrosleep therapy I. In: Wageneder FM, Germann RH, eds. Electrotherapeutic Sleep and Electroanaesthesia. Vol III. Third International Symposium in Varna. Graz: R M Verlag, 1974.

28. Rosenthal SH, Wulfsohn NL. Electrosleep—a clinical trial. Am J Psychiatry 1970;127:175-6.

29. Rosenthal SH, Wulfsohn NL. Electrosleep—a preliminary communication. J Nerv Ment Dis 1970;151:146-51.

30. Rosenthal SH, Calvert LF. Electrosleep: personal subjective experiences. Biolog Psychiatry 1972;4:187-90.

31. Nias DKB. Therapeutic effects of low-level direct electrical currents. Psychol Bull 1976;83:766-73.

32. Ryan JJ. Effects of transcerebral electrotherapy (electrosleep) on state anxiety according to suggestibility levels. Biolog Psychiatry 1976;11:233-8.

33. Rosenthal SH. Electrosleep: a double-blind clinical study. Biolog Psychiatry 1972;4:179-85.

34. Lewis SA, Oswald I, Evans JI, Akindale MO, Tompsett SL. Heroin and human sleep. Electroenceph Clin Neurophysiolog 1970;28:374-81.

35. Key DC. Human sleep during chronic morphine detoxification. Psychopharmacologia 1975;44:117-24.

36. Himmelsbach CK. Clinical studies of drug addiction. Physical dependence, withdrawal and recovery. Arch Intern Med 1942;69:766-72.

37. Ng LKY, Szara S, Bunney WE. On understanding and treating narcotic dependence: a neuropsychopharmacological perspective. Br J Addiction 1975;70:311-24.

38. Oswald I, Evans JI, Lewis SA. Addictive drugs cause suppression of paradoxical sleep with withdrawal rebound. In: Steinberg Hannah, ed. Scientific Basis of Drug Dependence. London: Churchill, 1969.

39. Kales A, Malmstrom EJ, Rickles WH, et al. Sleep patterns of a pentobarbital addict: before and after withdrawal. Psychophysiology 1968;5:208.

40. Adam K, Adamson L, Brežinová V, Hunter WM. Nitrazepam: lastingly effective but trouble on withdrawal. Br Med J 1976;1:1558-60.

41. Kales A, Scharf MB, Kales JD. Rebound insomnia: a new clinical syndrome. Science 1978;201:1039-41.

42. Patterson MA. The significance of current frequency in NeuroElectric Therapy (NET) for drug and alcohol

addictions. In: Wageneder FM, Germann RH, eds. Electrotherapeutic Sleep and Electroanaesthesia. Graz: R M Verlag, 1978:285-96.

43. Salmons S, Sréter FA. Significance of impulse activity in the transformation of skeletal muscle type. Nature 1976;263:30-4.

44. Stubbs DF. Frequency and the brain. Life Sci 1976;18:1-14.

7: What Is Addiction?

1. Lawrie Peter. Drugs: Medical, Psychological and Social Facts. London: Penguin, 1974.

2. Newsweek 1982 Dec 13:21.

3. Peele Stanton. Love and Addiction. New York: Taplinger Publishing Company Inc, 1975.

4. Brecher EM. Licit and Illicit Drugs. Boston: Little, Brown and Company, 1972:64.

5. Cocteau Jean. Opium: the Diary of an Addict. New York: Grove Press, 1958.

6. Jung Carl. Memories, Dreams, Reflections. Recorded and ed. by Aniela Jaffé. New York: Pantheon Books, 1963.

7. May Rollo. Love and Will. New York: WW Norton and Company Inc, 1969.

8. Tillich Paul. The Courage to Be. New Haven, Connecticut: Yale University Press, 1952.

9. O'Reilly. New insights into alcoholism. Time 1983 April 25:88-9.

10. Goldstein A. Heroin addiction. Sequential treatments employing pharmacologic supports. Arch Gen Psych 1976;33:353-8.

8: The Placebo Effect and Belief Systems

1. Smith Adam. Powers of Mind. New York: Random House Inc, 1975.

2. Cousins Norman. Anatomy of an Illness. New York: W W Norton and Company, 1979.

3. Coleman Vernon. The Medicine Men: Drug makers, Doctors and Patients. New York: Transatlantic Arts Inc, 1977.

4. Brewer Colin. World Medicine 1977 May 18.

5. Edwards J Guy. Antidepressants—yes or no? Br Med J 1978;1:110.

6. Ng LKY, Douthitt TO, Thoa NB, Albert CA. Modification of morphine-withdrawal syndrome in rats following transauricular electrostimulation: an experimental paradigm for auricular electroacupuncture. Biolog Psychiatry 1975;10:575-80.

7. Wen HL, Ho WKK, Ling N, Ma L, Choa GH. The influence of electroacupuncture on naloxone-induced morphine withdrawal. II. Elevation of immunoassayable beta-endorphin activity in the brain but not the blood. Am J Chinese Med 1979;7:237-40.

8. Marlatt GA, Rohsenow DJ. The think-drink effect. Psychology Today 1981; Dec:60-9.

9. Levine JD, Gordon NC, Fields HL. The mechanism of placebo analgesia. Lancet 1978;ii:654-7.

10. Galanter M, Diamond LC. Relief of psychiatric symptoms in evangelical religious sects. Br J Hosp Med 1981; Nov:495-8.

11. Berdyaev Nicolas. Freedom and The Spirit, 1935. New York: Irvington, 1982.

12. Frankl Victor. Man's Search for Meaning. New York: Pocket Books, 1963.

13. Tillich Paul. The Courage To Be. New Haven, Connecticut: Yale University Press, 1952.

14. Tillich Paul. The Meaning of Health. Richmond, California: North Atlantic Books, 1981;17-8,60.

9: The Spiritual Element in the Treatment of Addictions

1. Jung Carl. Modern Man in Search of a Soul. New York: Harcourt, Brace and Company, 1933.

2. Kelsey Morton. (Quoting Jung). Encounter With God. Minneapolis: Bethany Fellowship Inc, 1972.

3. Barclay William. New Testament Words. Philadelphia: The Westminster Press, 1976.

4. Koestler Arthur, Smythies JR. Beyond Reductionism: Alpbach Symposium 1968. New York: Macmillan, 1970.

5. Nicholi AM. The nontherapeutic use of

psychoactive drugs. A modern epidemic. N Engl J Med 1983;308:925-33.

6. Solzhenitsyn A. From Under the Rubble. South Bend IN: Regnery-Gateway Inc, 1981.

10: The Pharmakon Clinic and Marie Curie Research

1. Patterson MA. NeuroElectric Therapy: are endorphins involved? Mim's Magazine 1981;Sep:22-5.
2. Patterson MA. Effects of NeuroElectric Therapy (NET) in drug addiction: an interim report. UN Bull Narc 1976; 28:55-62.
3. Gallacher S. George Patterson on drug addiction and rehabilitation. Radix 1981;13:3-8.
4. Capel ID, Williams DC, Patterson MA. The amelioration of restraint stress by electrostimulation. IRCS Med Sci 1979;7:634.
5. Capel ID, Goode IG, Patterson MA. Tryptophan, serotonin and hydroxyindole acetic acid levels in rat brain following slow or fast frequency electrostimulation. IRCS Med Sci 1982;10:427-8.
6. Capel ID, Pinnock MH, Withey NJ, Williams DC, Patterson MA. The effect of electrostimulation on barbiturate-induced sleeping times in rats. Drug Dev Res 1982;2:73-9.
7. Capel ID, Pinnock MH, Patterson MA. The influence of electrostimulation on hexobarbital induced loss of righting reflex in rats. Acupuncture and Electro-Therapeutics Res, Int J 1982;7:17-26.
8. Moore RA. Dependence on alcohol. In: Pradhan SN, Dutta SN, eds. Drug abuse. Clinical and basic aspects. Saint Louis: The C V Mosby Company, 1977; 211-29.
9. Ho WKK, Wen HL, Ling N. Beta-endorphin-like immunoactivity in the plasma of heroin addicts and normal subjects. Neuropharmacology 1980; 19:117-20.
10. Pullan PT, Watson FE, Seow SSW, Rappeport W. Methadone-induced hypoadrenalism. Lancet 1983;i:714.
11. Dackis CA, Gurpegui M, Pottash ALC, Gold MS. Methadone induced hypoadrenalism. Lancet 1982;ii:1167.

12. van Praag HM. Depression. Lancet 1982;ii:1259-64.
13. Iversen LL. Neurotransmitters and CNS disease. Lancet 1982;ii:914-8.
14. Selye Hans. Stress Without Distress. Philadelphia, PA: J B Lippincott and Company, 1974.

11: The Pharmakon Clinic Treatment

1. Lawrie Peter. Drugs: Medical, Psychological and Social Facts. London: Penguin, 1974.
2. Jung Carl. Memories, Dreams, Reflections. Recorded and ed. by Aniela Jaffe. New York: Pantheon Books, 1963.
3. Frankl Victor. The Doctor and the Soul: From Psychotherapy to Logotherapy. New York: Random House Inc, 1973.
4. Hoffmann. Quoted by Lawrie P. In: Drugs: Medical, Psychological and Social Facts. London: Penguin, 1974.
5. Jung Carl. Ed. Man and His Symbols. New York: Doubleday and Company Inc, 1964.
6. Solzhenitsyn A. From Under the Rubble. South Bend IA: Regnery-Gateway Inc, 1981.
7. Temple Archbishop William. Readings from St. John's Gospel. London: Macmillan Publishers Ltd, 1961.

12: Independent Summary of NET; Clinical Research

1. Mitcheson M, Hartnoll R. Conflicts in deciding treatment within drug dependency clinics. In: West DJ, ed. Problems of drug abuse in Britain. Cambridge: Institute of Criminology, 1978:74-8.
2. Edwards G, Busch C. The partnership between research and policy. In: Edwards G, Busch C, eds. Drug problems in Britain. London: Academic Press, 1981:314-5.
3. Simpson DD. Treatment for drug abuse. Follow-up outcomes and length of time spent. Arch Gen Psychiatry 1981; 38:875-80.
4. Gomez E, Mikhail AR. Treatment of methadone withdrawal with cerebral electrotherapy (electrosleep). Br J Psychiatry 1979;134:111-3.

5. Catlin DH, Hui KK, Loh HH, Li CH. Pharmacologic activity of β-endorphin in man. Communications in Psychopharmacology 1977;1:493-500.
6. ©1983 by Omni Publications International Ltd., and reprinted with the permission of the copyright owner.

Postscript: Council of Europe Recommendations

1. Anonymous. Drink and drugs: double standards. The Economist 1982 Dec 4: 33-4.
2. Anonymous. An absence of alcohol policy (Editorial). Br Med J 1982;285: 1680-1.

Appendices I to XIX

1. Melzack R. The Puzzle of Pain. New York: Basic Books Inc., 1973.
2. Wen HL, Chau K. Status asthmaticus treated by acupuncture and electrostimulation. Asian J Med 1973;9:191-2.
3. Cooper IS, Riklan M, Snider S, eds. The Cerebellum, Epilepsy and Behavior. New York: Plenum Press, 1974: 229-44.
4. Ibid:217-27.
5. Illis LS. Experimental model of regeneration in the central nervous system. Brain 1973;96:47-60.
6. Huprich ST. Doctoral Dissertation, University of California at Los Angeles, 1975. Quoted by Liebeskind et al, 1976.
7. Rhodes DL. Doctoral Dissertation, University of California at Los Angeles, 1975. Quoted by Liebeskind et al, 1976.
8. Richardson DE, Akil H. Paper given at 7th Annual Meeting of the Neuroelectric Society, 1974.
9. Adam K, Adamson L, Brežinová V, Hunter WM. Nitrazepam: lastingly effective but trouble on withdrawal. Br Med J 1976;1:1558-60.
10. Akil H, Liebeskind JC. Monoaminergic mechanisms of stimulation-produced analgesia. Brain Res 1975;94:279-96.
11. Mayer DJ, Liebeskind JC. Pain reduction by focal electric stimulation of the brain—an anatomical and behavioral analysis. Brain Res 1974;68:73-93.
12. Kuhar MJ, Pert CB, Snyder SH. Regional distribution of opiate receptor binding in monkey and human brain. Nature 1973;245:447-50.
13. Richardson DE, Akil H. Paper given at 7th Annual Meeting of the Neuroelectric Society, 1974. Quoted by Liebeskind et al, 1976.
14. John ER, Kleinman D. "Stimulus generalization" between differentiated visual, auditory and central stimuli. J Neurophysiol 1975;38:1015-34.
15. Ramos A, Schwartz EL, Roy JE. Stable and plastic unit discharge patterns during behavioral generalization. Science 1976;192:393-6.
16. Patterson George N. Christianity and Marxism. Exeter, England: Paternoster Press, 1982.
17. Frankl Victor. The Doctor and the Soul: from Psychotherapy to Logotherapy. New York: Vintage Books, 1977.
18. Frankl Victor. Man's Search for Meaning: an introduction to logotherapy. New York: Pocket Books, 1963.
19. Tyrer P, Rutherford D, Huggett T. Benzodiazepine withdrawal symptoms and propanolol. Lancet 1981;i:520-2.
20. Simpson DD, Savage LJ. Drug abuse treatment readmissions and outcomes. Three-year follow-up of DARP patients. Arch Gen Psychiatry 1980;37: 896-901.
21. Inaba D. Needle therapy. The New York Times 1982 March 14:49(cols 2-4).
22. De Leon G. The role of rehabilitation. In: Nahas GG, Frick HC, eds. Drug abuse in the modern world. A perspective for the eighties. New York: Pergamon Press, 1981:298-307.
23. De Leon G, Wexler HK, Jainchill N. The therapeutic community: success and improvement rates 5 years after treatment. The Internat J Addictions 1982;17(4):703-47.
24. Tims FM. Evaluation of drug abuse treatment effectiveness: summary of the DARP followup research. Treatment Research Report for NIDA, 1982; DHSS publication no. (ADM)82-1194.
25. Lewis SA, Oswald I, Evans JI, Akindale MO, Tompsett SL. Heroin and human sleep. Electroenceph Clin

Neurophysiolog 1970;28:374-81.

26. Kales A, Scharf MB, Kales JD. Rebound insomnia: a new clinical syndrome. Science 1978;201:1039-41.

27. Lloyd G. I am an alcoholic. Br Med J 1982;285:785-6.

28. Kolb L, Himmelsbach CK. A critical review of the withdrawal treatments with method of evaluating abstinence syndromes. Am J Psychiatry 1938;94: 759-99.

29. Martin WR. Dependence on narcotic analgesics. In: Pradhan SN, Dutta SN, eds. Drug abuse. Clinical and basic aspects. Saint Louis: The C V Mosby Company, 1977;201-10.

30. Cushman P. Detoxification of methadone maintained patients. In: Schecter A, Alksne H, Kaufman E, eds. Drug abuse: modern trends, issues and perspectives. New York: Marcel Decker, Inc, 1978;337-45.

31. Smith CM. Pathophysiology of the alcohol withdrawal syndrome. Medical Hypotheses 1981;7:231-49.

32. Sutherland EW. Dependence on barbiturates and other CNS depressants. In: Pradhan SN, Dutta SN, eds. Drug abuse. Clinical and basic aspects. Saint Louis: The C V Mosby Company, 1977; 235-47.

33. Essig C. Barbiturate dependence. In: Harris RT, McIsaac WM, Schuster CR, eds. Advances in mental science II. Austin and London: University of Texas Press, 1970;129-40.

34. Kales A, Malmstrom EJ, Rickles WH et al. Sleep patterns of a pentobarbital addict: before and after withdrawal. Psychophysiology 1968;5:208.

35. Cowen PJ, Nutt DJ. Abstinence symptoms after withdrawal of tranquillising drugs: is there a common neurochemical mechanism. Lancet 1982;ii:360-2.

36. Peturrson H, Lader MH. Withdrawal reaction from clobazepam. Br Med J 1981;282:1931-2.

37. Tyrer P, Rutherford D, Huggett T. Benzodiazepine withdrawal symptoms and propanolol. Lancet 1981;i:520-2.

38. Law W, Petti TA, Kazdin AE. Withdrawal symptoms after graduated cessation of imipramine in children. Am J Psychiatry 1981;138:647-50.

39. Griffin N, Draper RJ, Webb MGT. Addiction to tranylcypromine. Br Med J 1981;283:346.

40. Huw J, Morgan C. Addiction to tranylcypromine. Br Med J 1981;283:618.

41. Cowe L, Lloyd DJ, Dawling S. Neonatal convulsions caused by withdrawal from maternal clomipramine. Br Med J 1982;284:1837-8.

42. Tennant FS, Rawson RA, McCann M. Withdrawal from chronic Phencyclidine (PCP) dependence with desipramine. Am J Psychiatry 1981;138: 845-7.

43. Parish P. Medicines. A guide for everybody. New York: Penguin Books, 1979: 47-50.

44. Tinklenberg JR. Abuse of marijuana. In: Pradhan SN, Dutta SN, eds. Drug abuse. Clinical and basic aspects. Saint Louis: The C V Mosby Company, 1977: 268-73.

45. Parish P. Medicines. A guide for everybody. New York: Penguin Books, 1979: 44-5.

46. Ellinwood EH, Petrie WM. Dependence on amphetamine, cocaine and other stimulants. In: Pradhan SN, Dutta SN, eds. Drug abuse. Clinical and basic aspects. Saint Louis: The C V Mosby Company, 1977:248-62.

47. Kelleher RT. Psychomotor stimulants. In: Pradhan SN, Dutta SN, eds. Drug abuse. Clinical and basic aspects. Saint Louis: The C V Mosby Company, 1977: 116-47.

48. Cohen S. Abuse of inhalants. In: Pradhan SN, Dutta SN, eds. Drug abuse. Clinical and basic aspects. Saint Louis: The C V Mosby Company, 1977: 290-302.

49. Golding J. Reported in: Smoking—a way to control arousal? The Journal (The Addiction Research Foundation of Ontario) 1981;10(March):4.

GLOSSARY

A layman's glossary of medical terms used in the text *(words in italic are defined elsewhere in the glossary).*

ACTH (adrenocorticotropic hormone): It is secreted by the pituitary gland in the brain to maintain *homeostatis* in many body functions. In response to environmental stress, there is increased release of ACTH into the circulation, which in turn rapidly stimulates the cortex of the adrenal gland to secrete more cortisol (or hydrocortisone) which prepares the organism for an emergency.

Action myoclonus: Spontaneous muscle spasms which occur only with attempted movements.

Acupuncture: Technique of medical treatment originating in China in which a number of very fine, metal needles are inserted into the skin at specially designated points.

Adrenalin: (epinephrine): Secretion of the medullary (central) part of the adrenal gland in response to strong emotions such as fear or anger, causing an immediate acceleration of bodily functions.

Afferent: Directed toward; as nerve impulses travelling from the periphery of the body inward to the spinal cord.

Agonist: A drug whose interaction with a *receptor* stimulates the usual biologic response.

Alpha rhythms: An *EEG* activity of 8 to 12 smooth, regular oscillations per second in subjects at rest.

Analgesia: Loss of pain sensation without loss of consciousness.

Anesthesia: Loss of pain sensation and also consciousness induced by chemicals.

Antagonist: A drug which interacts with the *receptor* but prevents the usual biologic response.

Ativan (lorazepam): A tranquilizer of the same chemical group as Valium (diazepam) and Librium (chlordiazepoxide).

Autonomic (nervous system): The division of the nervous system that regulates involuntary action, as of the intestines, heart, etc.

Aversive: Term used to indicate an adverse response to a drug instead of the usual desired or beneficial effects.

Biofeedback: A training technique in which an attempt is made to regulate a body function which is normally involuntary, such as heartbeat or blood pressure, by using instruments to monitor the function and to signal changes in it. Enables an individual to gain some element of voluntary control over autonomic body functions.

Cannula: A fine tube for insertion into a vein or other body or brain cavity.

Catecholamines: Cells capable of producing the catecholamine *neurotransmitters* such as norepinephrine, epinephrine (adrenalin), dopamine etc. They affect sleep, memory, food intake, movement, etc.

Carbon dioxide (CO_2) bottle-opener: A fine tube is pushed through the cork of a wine-bottle and CO_2 forced in from a cylinder under pressure, which results in ejection of the cork.

Cerebral anoxia: Lack of oxygen to the brain. This rapidly produces permanent damage to brain functions.

CNS (Central nervous system): Consists of the brain and spinal cord.

"Coke": Cocaine (slang).

Concha: The shell-like area of the ear near the external ear canal.

Corpus striatum: Part of the basal ganglia of the brain, probably involved in movement control and with perceptual information.

Cortical regulation: Control of certain body functions by the cortex, or outer surface of the brain.

Corticosterone and *cortisol* (or hydrocortisone): Corticosteroids secreted by the cortex of the adrenal glands, which are located on top of each kidney.

Cross-tolerance: *Tolerance* developed by using one drug, to another drug of a similar pharmacological structure.

Cryogenic surgery: Surgery by freezing in which a probe is inserted into the brain and the temperature of the tip is lowered to below freezing-point, destroying the cells causing the pathological condition.

Cutaneous: Pertaining to, or affecting the skin.

Darvon (propoxyphene): A pain-killing drug widely used by drug addicts.

Decerebrate rigidity: Rigidity of the body occurring when brain injury is so severe that it no longer controls the body.

D.T.s (delirium tremens): An acute delirium seen in alcohol withdrawal, characterized by trembling, confusion, nightmarish hallucinations, etc.

Double-blind: A research program for testing a new drug or treatment technique, where physicians, nurses, and patient are all unaware whether patients are receiving active treatment or the inactive *placebo*. Results of the testing are evaluated by scientists who are also unaware of which group received the active treatment and which the placebo. When the program has been completed, the secret code is broken, and the effects on those who received active treatment are compared with the effects on those receiving inactive placebo.

Dysphoria: Opposite of euphoria. Used to describe a state of feeling miserable and unwell, without being actually ill.

EEG (electroencephalogram): The recording of the brain's spontaneous electrical output, through several *electrodes* attached to the scalp.

Electrode: A metal or carbon rubber conductor which transmits electricity through the skin, such as is used in EEGs or EKGs.

Electrolytic: Pertaining to electrolysis, which uses a strong electric current to destroy cells.

Endogenous: Produced from within the body.

Endorphins: (A term, used in the text for the sake of simplicity and brevity, to include the group of enkephalins.) A family of opioid-like polypeptides found in many parts of the brain and body, which bind to the same *receptors* that bind *exogenous opioids*.

Enkephalin: The name given to the first "endorphin" discovered in 1975. The enkephalins are a group of pentapeptides with a much shorter duration of action than the endorphins.

Enzyme: A protein which acts as a catalyst in certain metabolic reactions; e.g., in breaking down enkephalin in the brain, or alcohol in the liver.

Ephedrine: A drug whose stimulating effects resemble those of adrenalin and amphetamines. Used mainly to relax the muscles in the bronchi during asthma attacks.

Etiology: The cause of a disease or disorder as determined by medical diagnosis.

Exogenous: Supplied from outside the body.

Facial or **7th cranial nerve:** Controls *lacrimation* and secretion from the nose and salivary glands, among other functions. Has a sensory connection with the ear.

"Free-basing": The dissolving of cocaine and the adding of chemical catalysts to precipitate out the pure chemical, which is then smoked (slang).

GABA (gamma-aminobutyric acid): An amino-acid which functions as an inhibitory *neurotransmitter* in all regions of the brain and spinal cord. May have a dual effect on food intake and may also be related to anxiety states.

Glossopharyngeal or **9th cranial nerve:** Carries sense of taste, etc., and is motor to pharyngeal muscles and to the parotid gland. Has a sensory connection with the ear.

Hashish: A purified extract made from the hemp plant and used as an hallucinogen.

Hepatic: Of the liver.

Heroin: An opioid prepared from morphine by acetylation. Produces a more powerful "high" (euphoria) than *morphine*.

Homeostatic: Pertaining to homeostasis, i.e., a state of physiological equilibrium produced by a balance of functions and of chemical composition within an organism.

Hormones: Chemical messengers that are carried in the blood a relatively long distance from their site of production in the body to the area they affect, e.g., insulin, estrogens, etc.

Hz (hertz): Cycles or pulses per second.

Hydration: To combine with water.

Ictal: Relating to a seizure, as in epilepsy.

Ictal EEG discharge: The firing of neurons caused by a seizure which shows in the *EEG*.

Infusion pump: A small pump which delivers a constant flow of a dissolved drug at a regular rate.

I.V. (intravenous): Injected into a vein. Called "mainlining" by addicts.

"Junk": Heroin (slang).

Lacrimation: Secretion of tears.

Laudanum: An alcoholic tincture of opium, widely used in Britain in the nineteenth century for relief of pain and discomfort.

Limbic lobe: A part of the brain which deals with memory storage and recall; may also control emotional behavior such as fear, rage, or motivation.

Mainlining: Term used by drug addicts for injection of drug into their veins.

Methadone: A synthetic *narcotic* which has *cross-tolerance* with *morphine* and *heroin*. It relieves the withdrawal symptoms of heroin addiction without giving the same "high" (though it is much harder to withdraw from than from heroin). Methadone is widely prescribed for heroin addicts in order to reduce drug-related crimes. It is also prescribed as an *I.V.* injection in Britain where it is called Physeptone.

Morphine: A compound extracted from the opium poppy and therefore called an opiate (or *opioid*). It relieves pain, and as a side-effect causes euphoria. Can be chemically altered to the more powerful heroin.

Myoclonus: Spontaneous muscle spasm or jerk.

Naloxone: A specific *antagonist* to all *opioid* drugs. Also an antagonist to the natural *endorphins*; this feature is often used clinically to detect endorphin activity.

Narcosis: See narcotic.

Narcotic: Any substance producing stupor associated with pain relief, such as the opiates or synthetic pain-killers.

Neuromodulators: Natural chemicals which alter neuronal function in various ways.

Neuron: A nerve cell.

Neurotransmitters: Chemicals made within the body to carry messages between nerve cells. They bridge the *synapse* and each one has a very specific function. Over forty have been isolated to date.

Noradrenaline (norepinephrine): An important *neurotransmitter* secreted by the medullary (central) part of the adrenal gland and also found throughout the brain and spinal cord. May be involved in the brain's "reward" system.

Opioids (previously used interchangeably with "opiates" which referred to opium and its derivatives): Various sedative *narcotics* containing opium or one or more of its derivatives, such as morphine, heroin, or codeine. The term now includes synthetic compounds having pharmacological effects similar to those of opium.

Periaqueductal grey: An area of the brain containing many *opioid receptors*.

Pharmakon: A Greek word meaning drugs, especially those that affect the mind; linked with sorcery in ancient times.

Placebo: An inert substance used as a control in "blind" experiments to assess the value of a drug or treatment.

Receptor: A specialized area on the surface of a cell to which either natural substances or *exogenous* drugs attach in order to effect their particular function.

Recidivism: Relapse to a former pattern of behavior such as substance abuse.

REM sleep: Rapid-eye-movement sleep, associated with dreaming. An essential part of normal sleep.

Reticular formation: An extensive network of nuclei and interconnecting fibers in the central part of the brain, which receives *afferent* impulses from many somatic, visceral, auditory, and visual sensory pathways, and relays these impulses to the appropriate areas in the brain. A fully alert state requires this network to be intact.

Restraint stress: Stress caused by enclosing an experimental animal in a specially designed cage.

Saline: Salt solution. "Normal saline" is sometimes used as the inert injection in *double-blind* trials.

Serendipity: The faculty of making fortunate, unexpected discoveries by accident.

Serotonin: An inhibitory *neurotransmitter* whose natural precursor is the essential amino-acid, tryptophan. Concerned with functions such as pain, sleep, mood-elevation, aggression, etc.

Serum: The fluid portion of the blood obtained after removal of the fibrin clot and blood cells.

Shakes: A coarse tremor of the hands, often seen in alcohol withdrawal. Milder than *D.T.s.*

"Smack": Heroin (slang).

Sniffing or **Snorting:** The inhaling of a drug up the nose from a special small spoon or through a roll of paper.

Somatic: Pertaining to the body, as distinguished from the mind.

Stereotactic surgery: A precise method of destroying a tiny portion of a deep-seated brain structure, located by use of three-dimensional coordinates; as, for example, to relieve the muscle tremors and rigidity of Parkinsonism.

Synapse (synaptic junction): The gap between nerve-cells. One neuron stimulates another to fire an electrical impulse by secreting a specific *neurotransmitter* into the gap between the cells.

TC (Therapeutic Community): A hostel for the long-term residential treatment of addicts who have stopped using drugs. An average stay is one to two years. They provide structured support of various kinds.

Thrombosis: Obstruction of an artery or vein by a blood clot forming on the vessel wall.

TM (Transcendental meditation): The practice of meditation by means of a "mantra," or arcane prayer-formula, used by a specific religious cult.

Tolerance: The need to progressively increase the dose of a drug in order to produce the effect originally achieved by a smaller dose.

Transepidermal inductive coupling: A receiver is surgically implanted beneath the skin to receive electrical signals from an electrode applied outside that skin area and connected to a special battery.

Trigeminal or **5th cranial nerve:** Sensory nerve for the face and motor to the jaws.

Vagus or **10th cranial nerve:** Controls many *autonomic* functions in the body such as the heart rate, breathing, and stomach and bowel functions. Has a sensory connection with the ear and the skin behind the ear.

Withdrawal: The mental and physical symptoms which occur when any type of drug, from heroin to nicotine, has been used regularly for some time and is then discontinued. (See Appendix XVIII, p.176 for details.)

CURRICULUM VITAE

Margaret Angus Patterson (née Ingram: Born 9th November 1922), M.B.E.,
M.B.Ch.B. (Aberdeen), F.R.C.S. (Edinburgh)

1944	Bachelor of Medicine and Surgery, University of Aberdeen, Scotland.
1944-45	Rotating Internship, Aberdeen Royal Infirmary and Sick Children's Hospital.
1945-47	Residency in Surgery in St. James' Hospital, Balham, London, under the tuition of Mr. Norman Tanner, Gastric and Oesophageal Surgeon.
1948	Fellow of the Royal College of Surgeons, Edinburgh, Scotland.
1948-53	Senior Lecturer in Surgery, Ludhiana Christian Medical College, and Surgeon to the College Hospital, Ludhiana, Punjab, India.
1954-56	Consultant Surgeon to various small hospitals in Northern India.
1957-61	Medical Superintendent of the Dooars and Darjeeling Tea Association Hospital, and Surgeon to the Hospital, N.E. India.
1961	Awarded Membership of the British Empire for medical services in India.
1962	Decorated with M.B.E. medal by Her Majesty the Queen in Buckingham Palace.
1964-73	Surgeon-in-Charge of the Surgical Unit of the Tung Wah Group Hospital, Hong Kong (850 beds).
1973-	Consultant in NeuroElectric Therapy for Addictions.

Publications (listed chronologically)

Patterson MA. Electro-acupuncture in alcohol and drug addictions. Clin Med 1974;81:9-13.

Patterson MA. Acupuncture and neuro-electric therapy in the treatment of drug and alcohol addictions. Aust J Alc Drug Dependence 1975;2:90-5.

Patterson MA. Addictions Can Be Cured. Berkhamsted, England: Lion Publishing, 1975.

Patterson MA. Effects of NeuroElectric Therapy (NET) in drug addiction: an interim report. UN Bull Narc 1976;28:55-62.

Patterson MA. The significance of current frequency in NeuroElectric Therapy (NET) for drug and alcohol addictions. In: Wageneder FM, Germann RH, eds. Electrotherapeutic Sleep and Electroanaesthesia. Graz: R M Verlag, 1978:285-96.

Capel ID, Williams DC, Patterson MA. The amelioration of restraint stress by electrostimulation. IRCS Med Sci 1979;7:634.

Patterson MA. NeuroElectric Therapy, enkephalin and drug addiction. In: International Review of Opium Studies. Philadelphia: Institute for Study of Human Issues 1981 (in press).

Patterson MA. NeuroElectric Therapy: are endorphins involved? Mim's Magazine 1981;Sep:22-5.

Capel ID, Pinnock MH, Withey NJ, Williams DC, Patterson MA. The effect of electrostimulation on barbiturate-induced sleeping times in rats. Drug Dev Res 1982;2:73-9.

Capel ID, Pinnock MH, Patterson MA. The influence of electrostimulation on hexobarbital induced loss of righting reflex in rats. Acupuncture and Electro-Therapeutic Res, Int J 1982;7:17-26.

Capel ID, Goode IG, Patterson MA. Tryptophan, serotonin and hydroxyindole acetic acid levels in rat brain following slow or fast frequency electrostimulation. IRCS Med Sci 1982;10:427-8.

Patterson Meg. Getting Off The Hook. Addictions Can Be Cured by NET (NeuroElectric Therapy). Wheaton Ill: Harold Shaw Publishers, 1983.

INDEX